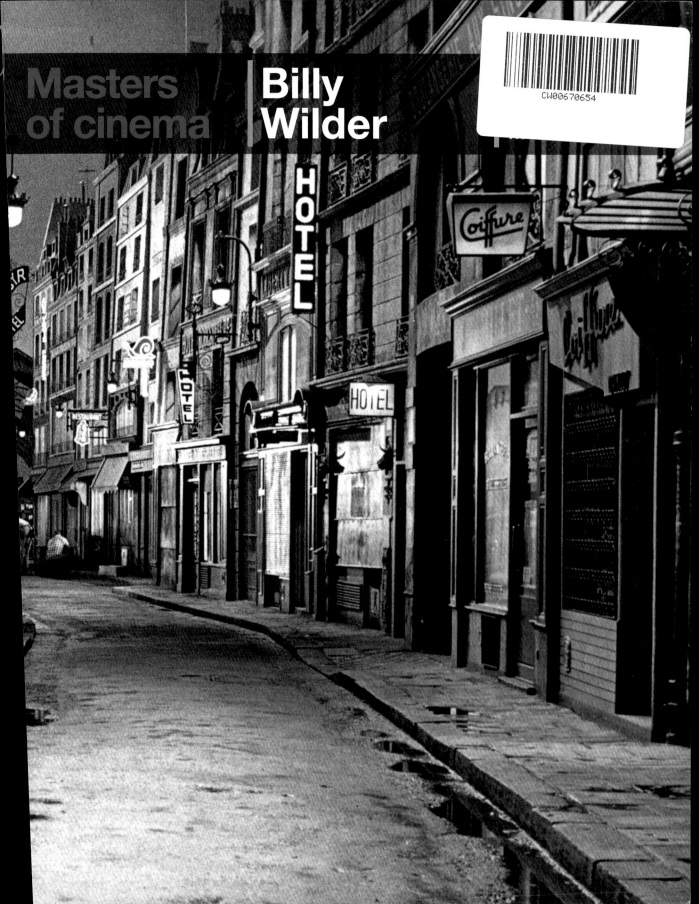

Masters
of cinema

Billy
Wilder

Contents

Marilyn Monroe in *The Seven Year Itch* (1955).

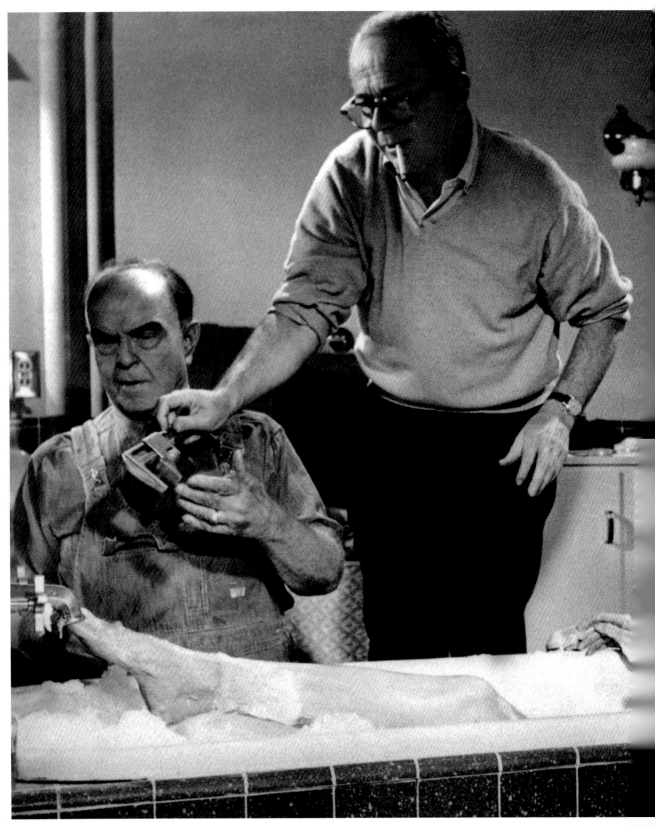

Introduction

Billy Wilder is acknowledged to be a master of American comedy. Regarded as the heir to Ernst Lubitsch, he was a director who pushed situation comedy to the edge of the absurd. His films have set generations of audiences laughing, and everyone remembers the hilarious misunderstandings suffered by the two male musicians in drag in *Some Like It Hot*.

Yet Wilder can't really be classified alongside the great classic directors of American comedy. His films are not like those of his contemporaries: he's less humane than Frank Capra, less refined than George Cukor and less abstract than Howard Hawks. His humour is darker and more disturbing, and his bold play on sexual ambiguities and innuendo-laden dialogue verge on the vulgar.

He looks at the world with a cynical eye, but he knows how to make people laugh. And that's not all, since he also made melodramas and film noir. His underlying subject matter is always the same, whether he's depicting the build-up to a murder, the cowardice of an alcoholic or of a gigolo drained of life by a star of the silent screen, the ridiculous adventures of a pair of musicians on the run from the Mafia or those of a naive cop turned unwilling pimp. Wilder may be portraying Lindbergh's solo flight across the Atlantic, the schemes of the occupying Americans in post-war Berlin or those of a Coca-Cola boss in cold war Berlin, but he's filming existential unease as well.

Whether his characters pretend to be little girls, English lords or women, devise scams or identity swaps, or prostitute themselves literally or figuratively, all ultimately encounter their moment of truth.

Every one of Wilder's films is a fable in which being bad is a dead end required by modesty and humour is a provocative politeness that highlights the baseness of things. Their social and ideological critiques reveal a tenderness that is hidden or betrayed. Obscenity appears as the necessary backwash of realism. For Wilder is above all a moralist.

Billy Wilder with Victor Moore and Marilyn Monroe on the set of *The Seven Year Itch* (1955).

From Waltztime to Wartime

From *Mauvaise Graine* to *The Lost Weekend*

'Every director has his own colours, like a painter. Some paint like Dufy, others are darker, like Soutine, say, but I've never wondered about whether I was bitter or cruel or pessimistic or anything. I like the story, that's all there is to it. I tell stories I like.'

Billy Wilder, 1962.

Billy Wilder in 1946.

Childhood in Vienna

Samuel Wilder was born to Jewish parents on 22 June 1906 in the town of Sucha Beskidzka, in Galicia, which at that time was a Polish province of the Austro-Hungarian empire. His father ran railway station restaurants and his mother looked after the children — they already had a two-year-old son called Wilhelm. Since visiting an uncle in the United States, Wilder's mother had been a fan of America, and she gave Samuel the nickname of Billy after Buffalo Bill, whose show she had enjoyed. The name stuck and was used by everyone.

Around 1909 the family moved to Vienna. The city was in the midst of a great renaissance in the theatre (Arthur Schnitzler) and painting (Egon Schiele). The mayor of Vienna was Karl Lueger, the founder of the Christian Social Party. He was anti-Semitic at a time when Jewish intellectuals were playing a major part in transforming the imperial capital into a centre of cultural activity. Chief among them were the psychoanalyst Sigmund Freud, composer Arnold Schönberg and journalist Karl Kraus.

Karl Lueger died in 1910, and the Social Democrats took over the running of the city. It was a period of mass movements and social unrest within the Austro-Hungarian empire. The annexation of Bosnia—Herzegovina in 1908 ultimately led to the outbreak of world war in 1914 and the dissolution of a world that Wilder would later gently caricature in *The Emperor Waltz* (1948), his only film to be set in Austria.

Wilder retained just two memories from those four years of war: queuing in the rain to buy potatoes, and the magnificent funeral of Emperor Franz Josef in 1916 — a contrast of deprivation with splendour that often inspired his later work.

The Armistice of 1918 put an end to the empire and redistributed its territories. Austria was declared a republic. In Vienna young Wilder was growing up and developing a taste for books, sport, cars, films, plays and jazz. His parents wanted him to become a lawyer — an indication of the degree to which Austrian Jews were socially integrated — but he wasn't interested in the bar and left university to become a journalist. In an interview he gave a picaresque account of his early days in that profession.[1] One Saturday in 1925, he walked into the offices of a newspaper and discovered the theatre critic having sex with his secretary. The man hired Wilder as his assistant. It sounds like a scene from one of his films — perhaps too much so to be true.

Verism in the Weimar Republic

When Wilder moved to Berlin in 1926, he discovered a pictorial movement that was at odds with Expressionism and New Objectivity: Verism, a movement that originated in Italy and that synthetized naturalism and realism while remaining firmly anchored in social issues. Its German proponents, including Georg Grosz, Otto Dix, Georg Scholz and Rudolph Schlichter, sought to identify the grotesque, farcical and picturesque aspects of human nature. Their works depict ugly, sleazy themes with dark humour and in a spirit of pessimistic criticism. Some Verists became political radicals and joined the Communist Party.

In an article on these angry young men in *Das Kunstblatt* in 1924, art historian Paul F. Schmidt wrote, 'It is an emphasis on a fanatical love of truth that does not want formal problems but seeks to speak directly about our present times, the chaotic aspect of a time of infamy, which they intend to defeat through brilliantly clear "objectivization". The unanimity to the point of "kitsch", deliberately "non-artistic" representation and observation of its own vices, emotional laziness and mediocrity that are thrown in the face of the bourgeoisie are simply intended to act like a supposedly unworked raw material. No surprise then that it flaps like a red rag exciting a bull.'

This movement came to an end around 1930, but Wilder retained traces of it, which leaked into his Hollywood dramas and comedies.

Left: Otto Dix, *Memory of the Halls of Mirrors in Brussels* (1920).

Right: Georg Grosz, *Promenade* (1922).

Having become a journalist, Wilder wrote about anything he was asked or permitted to comment on. While working for *Die Stunde*, he interviewed celebrities as part of an investigation into Mussolini. The composer Richard Strauss and playwright Arthur Schnitzler received him kindly, but Professor Sigmund Freud, who couldn't stand journalists, threw him out. None the less, Wilder felt it was an honour to have had any kind of encounter with Freud, even one of this sort.

At that period, Austria looked back on its past with nostalgia. Of the 700,000 square kilometres of territory held by the former empire, only 84,000 remained, while the country's population had dropped from 52 million to six million. To combat Pan-Germanism, the Treaty of Saint-Germain (1919) banned Austria from uniting with any province of Germany. Austria suffered a series of economic crises after the Armistice of 1918 and its social divisions were heightened by unemployment.

Anti-Semitism was brewing under the surface and fascist tendencies were gaining ground. Vienna was a lively city, but it could not compare with Berlin, and Wilder knew there would be opportunities for him in Germany. He met the jazz musician Paul Whiteman, who was about to give a concert in Berlin, and offered to write an article about the concert if Whiteman would pay for his trip. Whiteman agreed, and Wilder left Austria to settle in Germany, where he continued to work as a journalist. It was 1926, and he was twenty years old.

Berlin in the Roaring Twenties

Many cities left a mark on Wilder's life and he used them as settings for some of his films. Berlin was one of these. When he moved there it was a city in ferment in a country obsessed with nationalism. Populism and anti-Semitism were the weapons of choice for ideologues opposing the communists. *Mein Kampf* was published in 1925, but Hitler's

National Socialist party still seemed like a small group with no future.

The years of the Weimar Republic were artistically rich. From the modern designs of the Bauhaus to Max Reinhardt's experimental theatre, Stefan Zweig's novels, Gottfried Benn's poetry, Otto Dix's portraits and Paul Klee's abstracts, the arts were undergoing a transformation. German cinema was among the finest in the world, with 200 films produced annually. Fritz Lang had just made *Metropolis* (1927).

Some artists reacted against Expressionism and its phantoms[2] by adopting Verism, defined by Georg Grosz in 1925 as follows: 'The Verist holds up a mirror to his contemporaries so they can see what they look like. I was drawing and painting out of contradiction and trying through my work to convince people they were ugly, sick and deceitful.' Wilder adopted this point of view and explored the seedy, grotesque, farcical and picturesque sides of Berlin. Drugs and transvestites were all the rage, everyone was cooking up scams to work on everyone else, and overt prostitution and corruption were rife. Cynicism was a way of life. Wilder was more of a voyeur than a pervert and drew on whatever he found, even to the extent of becoming a gigolo (paid dancing partner) at the Eden Hotel in order to get material for an article.

His brother Wilhelm had emigrated to New York, where he had become a successful businessman. Their father went to visit him in 1928 and decided to move to America. He returned to Europe to collect his wife, travelled via Berlin to see Billy and died there from an intestinal occlusion. Wilder admired his father and the two shared a secret: his father had an illegitimate son, a half-brother Billy would never meet.

At this time Wilder was working for several newspapers: *Berliner Zeitung am Mittag*, *Tempo*, *Der Börsen-Kurier* and *Die Nachtsausgabe*. He wrote about sport, theatre and cinema, and even wrote a long article on the films of Erich von Stroheim, whose implacable realism fascinated him. He was also a ghostwriter on around fifty screenplays — melodramas, farces, comedies and crime stories — taking advice from Carl Mayer, scriptwriter of *The Cabinet of Dr Caligari* (1919), whom he used to meet in the mornings at the Café Kranzler. In 1929 his name appeared for the first time in film credits: for the screenplay of Ernest Laemmle's *Hell of a Reporter*. Wilder also frequented the Romanisches Café on Budapester Strasse, where he became friends with the Siodmak brothers. Robert was an assistant director, Curt a writer. Together the three made a film: *People on Sunday* (1930). In his book *Robert Siodmak, le maître du film noir*,[3] Hervé

Annie Schreyer and Brigitte Borchert in *People on Sunday* (1930).

Willi Forst, Willy Fritsch
and Lilian Harvey
in Paul Martin's
Ein blonder Traum (1932).

Opposite page: Michel Duran,
Raymond Galle and Pierre Mingand
in *Mauvaise Graine* (1934).

Dumont tells how Moriz Seeler set up Filmstudio 29 to produce it. He also gives details of the part played by Edgar G. Ulmer and Fred Zinnemann in making the film. It was Curt Siodmak who had the idea of filming the everyday lives of a few individuals during a Sunday in Berlin. These unknown men and women agreed to play their parts. According to some accounts, everything was improvised during the shoot and Wilder didn't write anything, or just swapped ideas with Robert Siodmak, whose apartment he shared. However, Wilder always claimed credit as the writer and the film is certainly conceived in the Verist spirit that emanates from all his films. Either way, *People on Sunday* was a critical success and UFA[4] gave Wilder a contract. The young writer was thinking of becoming a director himself and would go to the studios to watch films being made. In 1931 he saw Alfred Hitchcock make *Mary*, the German version of *Murder!*, one of his first talking films, full of experiments in sound.

When films began to talk, and particularly to sing, the Viennese operetta became a crucial model for German productions. Wilder followed orders, as did Robert Siodmak, with whom he worked on *Der Mann, der seinen Mürder sucht* (1931). From 1930 to 1933, he wrote screenplays for twelve films featuring stars of the day, including Lilian Harvey, Martha Eggerth, Willy Fritsch and Hans Albers. He had no illusions and wrote whatever was required. Some of these films were directed by Hans Steinhoff, who was to become famous through making the first Nazi propaganda film, *Hitler Youth Quex* (1933).

Now aged twenty-eight, Wilder was making good money and living in a pleasant apartment with furniture designed by Mies van der Rohe of the Bauhaus. He was a passionate sports fan, played poker, surrounded himself with women and collected works of art. Although he was a writer of commercial films, he was in contact with Bertolt Brecht, Walter Gropius and other members of the Berlin intelligentsia.

But, while German audiences were laughing and swooning as the charming film stars sang, a nightmare was coming true in their country. In 1930 Hitler's National Socialist party won 107 seats in the Reichstag. By 1932 they had 230. On 3 March 1933 their numbers swelled to 288 and on 12 November of the same year they became the only party in the parliament.

Fame, money and social success had not robbed Wilder of insight, and he did not wait until that moment to act. On the day after the Reichstag fire of 27 February 1933 he sold everything he owned and fled to Paris with his current girlfriend.

A Parisian interlude

Paris was new to Wilder and he was happy there; he later set several of his films in the city. Other people from the film world had also fled Berlin, and together they formed a little colony at the Hotel Ansonia. Besides Wilder, it was home to the actor Peter Lorre and musicians Franz Waxman and Frederik Hollander, with whom he would later work in Hollywood.

The French and German film industries had close commercial and artistic links at that time. The same film might be shot simultaneously in both languages, with different actors and sometimes different directors. But while the fugitives from Germany could easily find work in Paris as directors or technical crew, there was less demand for the actors and scriptwriters. Wilder wrote screenplays that nobody wanted. The director Joe May put one of them, *Pam Pam*, in his suitcase when he set off for the USA, but it was never made.

Still, Wilder had learned French in school and spoke it well enough to make one film in France, *Mauvaise Graine* ['Bad Seed'] (1934), a story of car thieves. With its encounter between people from different social backgrounds, role playing and trickery, it already reflects all Wilder's themes. He directed the film with Alexandre Esway (1898–1947), a director of Hungarian origin who had recently moved to France. Wilder later remembered the shoot: 'I don't remember how we found the money. It was kind of in the cinema verité genre about the kind of vitelloni who steal cars. It wasn't all that bad, but there were lots of chase sequences and we didn't have the money to pay for transparencies. In other words the camera and lights were on a truck and it was pretty dangerous.'[5] The film has real documentary beauty: the city of Paris is shot in a way that offers a fore-taste of the style brought to prominence by the filmmakers of the French New Wave. At that time, only Jean Renoir was working in this way.

But *Mauvaise Graine* is not all realistic snapshots of urban life. It is a fable that heralds Wilder's future style with its touches of *cinéma vérité* combined with the formulas of farce and clichés from adventure films.

It tells the story of a rich kid who discovers real life with a bunch of conmen and experiences sincere friendship and love, all depicted without a trace of mawkishness. While each character is acting a part, for himself as well as others, we can see the Verist elements that were present in the earlier *People on Sunday*. Wilder also displays an amazing sense of rhythm and pace. His film is built on cadence and we sense the director's love of sport and jazz. It's all about energy in action. There are even echoes of avant-garde experimentation in this production intended for a mass audience, while the female lead is a seventeen-year-old by the name of Danielle Darrieux.

Hollywood screenwriter

After this experience, Wilder crossed the Atlantic. The American studio bosses were not pleased by the sudden influx of emigrés from Mitteleuropa, although they had enticed foreign talent to join them ten years previously in order to stifle competition. At that time directors (Paul Leni, Ernst Lubitsch, Friedrich Wilhelm Murnau) and actors (Emil Jannings) had left Germany to make their careers in Hollywood.

When the talkies arrived, many such actors had gone back home because their English wasn't very good. Then the stock market crash of 1929 and subsequent depression had led the studios to focus on producing entertainment films that were ill-suited to the ambitions of UFA-trained directors.

This was the context that met the exiles of the 1930s on their arrival. While some, like Fritz Lang, managed to work on major films, others took a while to get established (Robert Siodmak, Otto Preminger), or survived by making B movies (Ewald A. Dupont, Wilhelm Thiele, Edgar G. Ulmer). Anyone who was not a musician or a technician had trouble finding work, particularly if, like Wilder, they didn't speak English. There was a small group of German-speakers in Hollywood who supported their compatriots — directors Ernst L. Frank, Joe May and Wilhelm Thiele all hired Wilder as an additional scriptwriter on some of their films. But contracts were few and far between.

Wilder learned the language of the country, used his experience as a journalist to study American behaviour and wrote stories that he tried to sell to the studios. After uncredited work on the dialogue of Raoul Walsh's *Under Pressure* (1935), he went back to see his mother in Vienna, where, worryingly, he found the Jewish community apparently unaware of the danger from Nazi Germany. On returning to Hollywood, he was hired by Paramount.

Paramount was a major studio where Cecil B. DeMille, Ernst Lubitsch and Josef von Sternberg[6] were making significant films. Wilder had no idea he would become one of its most respected figures and direct its greatest stars, including Marlene Dietrich, Maurice Chevalier and Gary Cooper.

A manager in the screenwriting department had the idea of putting Wilder to work with Charles Brackett, a very different personality who made no secret of his reactionary traditionalism. Despite this, the two hit it off and became established as a comedy-writing duo. They came to the attention of the German director Ernst Lubitsch, who hired them to work on *Bluebeard's Eighth Wife* (1938) and then on *Ninotchka* (1939). Lubitsch had moved to Hollywood in 1923 and was now a powerful force. His many box-office successes made him one of Paramount's most important directors, known as 'the King of comedy'.

Lubitsch had a crucial influence on the way Wilder later directed comedies: 'I started out working with Brackett, then along came Lubitsch; he didn't have a single writer's credit to his name, but he did a lot. He was the only one who could add the "Lubitsch touch". We used to bring him ideas, he'd say yes or no and then he'd throw in some of his own. For example, Brackett, Walter Reisch and I had worked for weeks, wondering how we could show that Garbo, in *Ninotchka*, was becoming a bourgeois woman, that she was starting to get interested in the products of capitalism.[...] We'd written loads of stuff, then one day Lubitsch said, "We'll do a scene with the hat." So

Pierre Mingand and Danielle Darrieux in *Mauvaise Graine* (1934).

Alexander Granach, Greta Garbo, Felix Bressart and Sig Rumann in Ernst Lubitsch's *Ninotchka* (1939).

we see her arrive at the beginning, with the three commissars, and she goes past a shop window in which she sees a very fancy hat. She says, "How can a civilization survive when women put hats like that on their heads? It's the end of capitalism!" Then we see her going past the window and she goes, "Ha ha!" Then later she sends the three commissars out of her room, shuts her door, opens her cupboard, takes out the hat, puts it on her head and looks in the mirror. That's pure Lubitsch, total simplicity. And it's not a writer's idea, it's primarily a visual idea.'[7]

From 1938 to 1942 the duo wrote eight comedy screenplays. Wilder's name appeared alone only on the credits of *Rhythm on the River* (1940), as author of the original story written in Berlin a few years earlier.

Charles Brackett and Billy Wilder were soon respected writers who could bring tragedy into fantasy, dared to write innuendo-laden dialogue and brought the genre up to date while retaining the fizz of the Viennese operetta or the hidden seriousness of Schnitzler's plays.

This orientation set them apart from the sophisticated current dominated by George Cukor (*The Philadelphia Story*, 1940) and the social satires of Frank Capra (*You Can't Take It with You*, 1938). They were closer to the burlesque farce of Howard Hawks's *Bringing up Baby* (1938), and indeed Hawks had brought them in during the writing of *Ball of Fire* (1941).

After receiving an Oscar nomination in 1939 for their screenplay for *Ninotchka*, Wilder and Brackett were nominated again in 1941 for Mitchell Leisen's *Hold Back the Dawn* (1941), made by a director who had started out as a costume designer on Cecil B. DeMille's films. Brackett and Wilder had previously written the screenplay for Leisen's *Midnight* (1937), a film that in subject matter and mischievous tone foreshadows in many ways the comedies Wilder went on to make.

At the request of Paramount, which kept them pigeonholed as comedy writers, the duo worked with Leisen again on *Arise My Love* (1940).

In reality Wilder wasn't feeling much like laughing at this time. He had not had news of his family since the annexation of Austria by Nazi Germany in 1938 and he was going through a difficult period in his personal life. In late 1936 he had married Judith Cappicus and in 1939 she gave birth to twins, Victoria and Vincent, but

Vincent died eight weeks later. Moreover, Wilder was finding his work as a screenwriter frustrating, as writers had no power to ensure that their work was respected. Directors and stars would change the script in any way they choose. Relations with Leisen were particularly difficult, since he banned writers from his sets. On hearing that Charles Boyer had refused to play the opening scene of *Hold Back the Dawn*, in which he had to tell his story to a cockroach, Brackett and Wilder cut his lines and took him out of the last part of the film altogether. This revenge says much about the irritation felt by the two writers.

Howard Hawks did not share the attitude of his colleagues. He was pleased with the screenplay of *Ball of Fire* and invited Wilder to come on set. Wilder was present throughout the filming and analysed the way Hawks's working methods differed from those he had seen in Berlin and Paris. They impressed him so much that he decided to go back to directing.

From screenplay to screen

At that time very few screenwriters went on to direct, no doubt because such an accumulation of roles would have reduced the influence of the producers over their films. Only Preston Sturges had recently managed to pull it off.

Wilder was given the go-ahead to try, but he asked to remain a screenwriter as well. Knowing that a commercial flop would end his directing career, he wrote a comedy — *The Major and the Minor* (1942) — at a time when he had nothing to laugh about. He was getting information about the persecution of the Jews in Europe and feared the worst for his family. But humour is the politeness of despair and farce was a way of discreetly concealing his concern.

Just before shooting started, Wilder sought advice from Ernst Lubitsch, who told him that he himself panicked before starting every film. Fritz Lang was more pragmatic and suggested he should go for the best directors of photography. Wilder followed this advice, working with John Seitz, Charles Lang, Jr, Joseph LaShelle, Ernst Lazlo, Russell Harlan and Gerry Fisher.

The casting of *The Major and the Minor* didn't go as Wilder would have wished. Fred Astaire's former dancing partner Ginger Rogers agreed to star, which was a great advantage, since she had just

Ginger Rogers in *The Major and the Minor* (1942).

won an Oscar and was riding high in the box office. So Wilder wanted the biggest male comedy star to play opposite her and asked for Cary Grant, who had held that position since his success in Cukor's *The Philadelphia Story* (1940) and Hawks's *Bringing up Baby* (1938) and *His Girl Friday* (1940). But the studio refused and imposed Ray Milland, who was on a contract with Paramount. In every other respect Wilder was left to his own devices. No one understood the subversive nature of his screenplay: a woman disguises herself as a girl of twelve and in that role seduces a man. The censors didn't notice the metaphor of paedophilia any more than they understood that Wilder was scratching the surface of American society and showing men, young and old, as immature.

The Major and the Minor is not a great film. It is directed without visual flair — Wilder had not yet mastered the art of movements in space and everything relies on dialogue that perpetuates misunderstandings. But these are minor faults compared to the film's furious pace, while his direction of the actors reflects the beneficial influence of Lubitsch and Hawks in relation to timing. Audiences were greatly entertained by this story of disguise in which imposture becomes a tool in the search for truth.

The film's success obliged Paramount to give Wilder a director's contract and he went on to shoot *Five Graves to Cairo* (1943), a contribution to the war effort imposed on the studios by the government. The problem was that Wilder didn't want to film battles and a simple struggle between good and evil for propaganda purposes; so he wrote a spy story based on Lajos Biro's play *Hotel Imperial*. To retain control of the film, he asked Brackett to produce it. Then he got Erich von Stroheim to play the part of Field Marshal Rommel, realizing his desire to work with a man he admired. The two became great friends.

Loyal to his old companions, Wilder wanted Franz Waxman to write the score for the film, but he wasn't available — in a few years Waxman had risen to prominence in Hollywood, working with Frank Borzage, Alfred Hitchcock and Victor Fleming. In his place Wilder chose the Hungarian

Diana Lynn and Ginger Rogers in *The Major and the Minor* (1942).

Following pages: Anne Baxter and Erich von Stroheim in *Five Graves to Cairo* (1943).

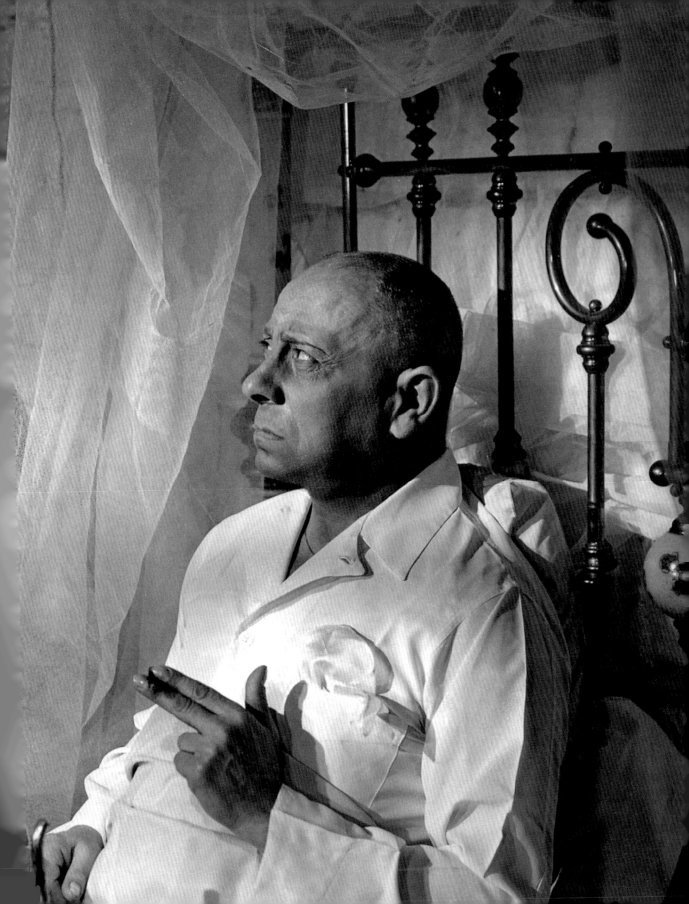

Barbara Stanwyck and Fred MacMurray in *Double Indemnity* (1944).

composer Miklos Rozsa, who had come to the USA with the producer Alexander Korda. Their meeting proved crucial and Rozsa became one of Wilder's favourite collaborators.

As Wilder himself has said, *Five Graves to Cairo* is the first film in which he shows a mastery of cinematic style, using devices that would reappear in different variations throughout his career. The film opens with a tank driving aimlessly through the desert after a battle, telling us that this will be a story about solitary wandering towards survival, both for the free world fighting against Nazism and for the character caught up in a game with death.

The action continues in a hotel, an enclosed space in which everyone tells lies, hides what they are really thinking and falls victim to deception. There are no heroes here, just a morbid, suffocatingly seedy atmosphere that is always realistic and never dreamlike.

Five Graves to Cairo was the film that first revealed Wilder's dark side, which would be fully expressed through his films noirs and melodramas and often remains present in his wildest comedies.

Darkness triumphs

The year 1944 saw the release of several films that crystallized a new trend: film noir. Its makers were generally of European origin and made melodramas and thrillers in a style strongly influenced by the formal experimentation of the pre-Nazi

Fred MacMurray and Edward G. Robinson in a deleted scene of *Double Indemnity* (1944).

German cinema, in which naturalism combines with more nightmarish qualities. These pessimistic films often show a dramatic structure influenced by Orson Welles's *Citizen Kane* (1941), using voice-overs and flashbacks.

Wilder adopted this approach in *Double Indemnity* (1944), adapted from a short story by James Cain.[8] His co-writer Charles Brackett was uninspired by the sleazy subject and was replaced by Raymond Chandler,[9] who wrote a screenplay that overturned the stereotypes of the crime thriller. The relationship between the co-writers was not easy, with Chandler feeling that Wilder treated him as a subordinate. Nevertheless they worked effectively together. Wilder was deeply impressed by Chandler's phrase 'Nothing ever looks emptier than an empty swimming pool.'

Double Indemnity is a film told by the murderer, constructed around his journey towards the crime like a news report with hints of the confessional. Here again, we find a change of identity, lies and gloom. Each character creates a scenario in order to commit or denounce a crime motivated by sex and money. But they all get caught in the machinery.

Wilder hired Barbara Stanwyck, whom he had met on the set of *Ball of Fire*, along with iconic thriller actor Edward G. Robinson, but gave them roles that were polar opposites of the character types they usually played. In the same way he chose a comedy actor, Fred MacMurray, to play

the main character, the anti-hero whose job is to unmask insurance cheats, but who turns it on its head to become a conman and a murderer.

This kind of inversion would become Wilder's trademark. He launched his approach in a subtly nuanced way that enabled him to trick the censors. For *Double Indemnity* is not just a cruel film about the temptation to commit crime, it is also a critique of the American way of life and the failures of a system based on money and success. The colourful dialogue and bitterly violent reversals of fortune bring impeccable pace to an oppressive film in which the key character is not the bad girl in a blonde wig played by Stanwyck, nor her accomplice, but the one played by Robinson, a man who decodes their machinations by means of statistics, trusting to his instinct and his intelligence. He is obsessed with the idea of inexorably carrying out what he regards as his mission. In a way he is the double of Wilder and is (almost) never fooled by appearances. This renders him lucid to the point of cynicism, although he is blinded by affection for his colleague. The darkness of the world is so familiar to him that he has become definitively pessimistic.

Once the film was in the can, Wilder decided to take out the last two sequences showing the guilty man's trial and execution, on the grounds that they added nothing to the overall effect. *Double Indemnity* was a critical and popular success. Wilder received Oscar nominations for Best Screenplay and Best Director.

Not wanting to be categorized in any particular genre, he avoided making another crime story, bought the rights to a novel about alcoholism and adapted it with Charles Brackett under the title *The Lost Weekend* (1945).

This film is again constructed around a voice-over and flashbacks. Like *Double Indemnity*, it is the sordidly confessional story of a descent into hell, realistically filmed, in which Wilder muddies the waters in order to avoid pathos or a clinical depiction of dependency. So the narrator's first hallucination appears as a subjective image. As an opera chorus sings the drinking song from *La Traviata*, the character played (against type) by Ray Milland sees his raincoat in the cloakroom, in which he has concealed a bottle of whisky. Wilder places the

Fred MacMurray and Barbara Stanwyck in *Double Indemnity* (1944).   23

Billy Wilder and film noir

It was not his comedies that established Wilder as a Hollywood director, but his films noirs. The success of *Double Indemnity* helped establish the film noir movement, which had been building for a long time and reached its peak in 1944 with the release of other films by Mitteleuropean directors: Otto Preminger's *Laura*, Robert Siodmak's *Phantom Lady* and Fritz Lang's *The Woman in the Window*. Each of these films showed the influence of the Germanic style and the stamp of its *auteur*, and in them sleaze took different forms. Preminger combined it with icy sophistication while Siodmak and Lang included dreamlike elements or references to psychoanalysis. Wilder meanwhile opted for a disturbing realism and to this end hired Raymond Chandler, a writer from the literary school of the *Black Mask*. His concern to give a crime fiction the air of reportage made his film appear as a reflection of reality and denied it any romanticism. His pair of crooks thus become all the more fascinating – they are ordinary, human monsters. He used the same approach in his dramas *The Lost Weekend* (1945), *Sunset Boulevard* (1950), *Ace in the Hole* (1951) and *Witness for the Prosecution* (1957), and it was later crystallized in *Fedora* (1978), a melodrama of brooding darkness associated with the end of another illusion, that of traditional romantic cinema. Wilder established sleazy realism, one of the essential concepts of film noir, but he also deployed it so well in other works that it adds a moral nuance to the confessions of the evil-doers and cowards who fill all his films. Knowing that film noir can never work in direct conjunction with comedy, he retained its principles in a concealed form, enhancing his social and burlesque farces with a cynical pessimism that always overarches the interplay of misunderstandings and comic situations. In this way he was able to make cruel satires using elements normally seen as disgusting or frightening. *The Apartment* (1960) is the most accomplished prototype of a film noir, disguised in a sombre humour, caustic and almost unbearably nasty. Conversely, when Wilder makes a gangster film – *Some Like It Hot* (1959) – parody prevails, since the genre is too coded to be subverted in that way. Lastly, if Wilder often copies fairy tales, it's because he understands that, to borrow Jean Cocteau's words, 'Fairy tales are the erotic novels of children because they frighten them' and that a clown's grimace is really more frightening than funny. Like a film noir, sarcasm is diabolical.

Opposite page: Ray Milland in *The Lost Weekend* (1945).

Following pages: Barbara Stanwyck, Fred MacMurray and Edward G. Robinson in *Double Indemnity* (1944).

mental image on a theatre stage, which, combined with the narrator's profession as a writer (hence a person of imagination), undermines the medical reality of the hallucination. After this we are slyly distanced from the character. Later Wilder shows another drunk suffering from delirium tremens. The scene takes place in a hospital and the man screams and struggles against animals we cannot see. Conversely, the narrator is shown charmed by the appearance of a bat and a rat when he has his own first attack. It is the sight of their sudden mutual destruction that makes him scream, rather than fear that they will turn on him.

These scenes turn the medical illustration of delirium tremens on its head. For the narrator sees his hallucination 'as a show', as the screen reveals it to us. The hallucinations of the patient assailed by invisible animals are frightening, but those of the writer are not; he seems to 'give himself' up to the hallucination with pleasure. Things we can see are always less frightening than things we can't. The bloody hallucination watched by the narrator is less disturbing than the realistic reconstruction of the alcoholics' ward in the hospital. This oppressive sequence, like those with the pawnshop owner or the barman, portrays alcohol as a social evil. It is a means of alienation through lack or excess, a dependency controlled by the government, which has grown rich on it following the end of Prohibition.

The Lost Weekend does not show that alcohol brings about a harmful disconnection from reality, but that people who drink are in tune with the far more horrible reality of their own cowardice. The *mise-en-scène* endlessly condemns the character for his spinelessness rather than his vice.

This approach, moralist rather than moralizing, disturbed the Paramount bosses, particularly as the preview audiences found the film depressing. Meanwhile a spirits manufacturer offered to buy the film to prevent its release. But Wilder paid little attention to all this. The war had just finished and he went to Europe with a division of the American army, where he learnt that his family had been deported and exterminated in Auschwitz. He then supervised the editing of a documentary on the concentration camps, *The Death Mills* (1945). The confirmation that the worst had occurred increased his pessimism.

Later Wilder responded with bitter, provocative irony to the observation that he was the only director in Hollywood whose family had died in an extermination camp: 'You've got optimists and pessimists. The first died in the gas chambers. The others have swimming pools in Beverly Hills.'

Sniping at Targets
From *The Emperor Waltz* to *The Fortune Cookie*

Joan Fontaine and Bing Crosby in *The Emperor Waltz* (1948).

A time of ghosts

On his return from Germany in 1946, Wilder received two Oscars for *The Lost Weekend* (screenplay and directing) while Ray Milland picked up Best Actor. Then, and to everyone's amazement, having won acclaim as an *auteur* of dark, serious films, Wilder proceeded to make a musical comedy in colour. The genre was then in vogue and all the studios were making them. Wilder chose to follow suit to hide his distress at all that he had just seen in Europe.

The Emperor Waltz (1948) is set in Austria in the early twentieth century. Its depiction was less sparkling than the usual run of stories set in Vienna, since the screenplay overturns the classic principle of fairy stories in which the prince marries the shepherdess. Here an aristocratic Prussian lady falls in love with an American salesman who is trying to sell the emperor a gramophone. Their dogs feel a similar, parallel passion, which results in mongrels. The star, Bing Crosby, sings pleasant melodies in glorious Technicolor. Everything seems to conform to tradition, except that the film functions through a structure of flashbacks — a lady of the court is telling the story to her friends. Wilder also plays with a device he would often use, the contrast and mutual attraction between representatives of diametrically opposed worlds.

But this film is also about the reincarnation of ghosts. Each character is the image of a period that has vanished, from the members of the Imperial court to the Austrian peasants and the American gramophone salesman. In terms of style, the reference to German musical comedies made during the Weimar Republic also points to a kind of film entertainment that had disappeared under Hitler.

The Emperor Waltz is the first film in a 'ghost' trilogy. Its spectres are those of an apparent good life. The next film would feature the ghost of Nazism, emerging in a ruined Germany.

A Foreign Affair (1948) was one of several propaganda films to depict the occupation of a defeated Germany by American troops. These films were designed to promote the image of the American army, but Billy Wilder does not go along with the consensus, instead transforming the concept into vitriolic satire by establishing a bizarre *ménage à trois* between an American officer, a former Nazi and a naive Republican congresswoman from Iowa on an official inspection visit to Berlin. Daily life among the ruins is all black-market deals, fraternization and fornication with German women,

scheming, greed and selfishness. This is a comedy of manners conveying a raw, squalid realism that transforms vaudeville into sarcastic satire.

The most important aspect of the film is not to be found in the comedy of its situations, the manipulation of the gallant American woman, nor the libertine cynicism of the soldier in charge of denazification, who fakes reality so he can have a good time. It lies in the fact that Marlene Dietrich's character is a ghost of Nazism (in news-reels she is shown with Hitler) acting as bait to lure back to the surface (on screen) a Nazi thought to be dead. She is also the ghost of the 'Blue Angel',[10] who had her moment of glory under the Third Reich and draws to herself all that remains of that accursed time.

Yet this dangerous woman is not portrayed as a monster or a bitch. She is human, not some Manichaean caricature. This was very important to Wilder, who fell out with Charles Brackett over this point during the writing of the screenplay. For Wilder's strength is to portray villains, idiots, impostors, cowards and murderers and to turn them into human beings. This is a highly disturbing process. He reveals the underlying nature of individuals and the hazards of idealism.

This same process was at work in Wilder's next film, to the irritation of Brackett, who wanted to give the comedy treatment to their new subject, the story of love between an unscrupulous young screenwriter and a star of the silent era who is now a shadow of her former self. Wilder did not give in

The kiss between Jean Arthur and John Lund

A Foreign Affair

Seduction and lies are recurrent themes in Wilder's films. In *A Foreign Affair* both are conveyed through images that are at once theatrical and cinematic. Jean Arthur and John Lund are in the room used to store compromising archives. To prevent the young woman from finding the file he wants to remain hidden, the man decides to seduce her. He opens the filing cabinet drawers one by one, hemming her in until he has her completely imprisoned and can kiss her. The inversion principle dear to Wilder is simple here. The man opens the drawers he doesn't want the woman to look into in order to prevent her exploring them. In so doing he obliges her to move her body rather than use her mind. So, with each drawer that's opened, the woman gets further away from researching another woman's compromising past and comes closer to a present moment in which her body will be offered to the man, who is using this trick to direct her while simultaneously making her the rival of the woman whose file she is looking for.

Opposite page: Marlene Dietrich in *A Foreign Affair* (1948).

John Lund and Jean Arthur in *A Foreign Affair* (1948).

to his partner and *Sunset Boulevard* (1950) is a radically pessimistic tragedy.

However, the original screenplay included an idea whose realization harmed the film at the preview screenings. It opened with a discussion between corpses in a morgue. Audiences found this ridiculous so Wilder cut the sequence, which had sabotaged the film's tragic tone, but kept the principle of a flashback with a dead narrator heard speaking over a score by Franz Waxman, whom he had hired once more after working with Miklos Rozsa (*Five Graves to Cairo*, *Double Indemnity*, *The Lost Weekend*) and Frederik Hollander (*A Foreign Affair*).

Although Wilder kept moving from one film genre to another to avoid being classified in any of the industry's categories, it becomes increasingly clear that all his characters are similar in personality and behaviour. With this ghost trilogy certain constants become apparent: differences of social situation, motivation and, crucially, ways of understanding reality; role play and lies; cowardice and a lack of lucidity; and manipulation of some by others. And always there is a discomfort with one's life, past and present.

Norma Desmond, the former star of *Sunset Boulevard*, lives with ghosts, and lies to herself about what she has become by watching films in which she is forever young. She also lies to herself about the feelings and motivations of her screenwriter gigolo and about her own professional superiority to Cecil B. DeMille, refusing to acknowledge her lies and embalming herself in her dream without realizing that it is a destructive nightmare.

Everyone else lies to her out of pity, self-interest and even love (her servant Max, who was her first husband when he was a great director). So she has the illusion of reigning in the enclosed world of her mind and of her house, which is entered by only an undertaker for the funeral of a pet chimpanzee, former stars of the silent era, who themselves look like ghosts, and a young man who is sufficiently weak and greedy to cynically plunge her deeper into her neurosis.

Everyone feeds on everyone else in this insane, masochistic psychodrama in which role

Gloria Swanson in *Sunset Boulevard* (1950).

Following pages: Gloria Swanson and Cecil B. DeMille in *Sunset Boulevard* (1950).

play is a way of speeding up the dance of death, turning it into a devouring vortex. The counterpoint of ordinary life is the screenwriter's relationship with the girl who is secretly working with him, which simply heightens the oppressive malaise generated by watching this film.

All these elements are already enough to make it a masterpiece, but Wilder has the brilliance to add a dimension of reality by having several of the characters play themselves, including not only Buster Keaton and Cecil B. DeMille, but also, in an obvious projection, Gloria Swanson, who, like Norma Desmond, had been a star of the silent screen, and Erich von Stroheim, a director destroyed by Hollywood, as Max was. Moreover, it had been his entanglements with Swanson on *Queen Kelly* (1928) that had brought about von Stroheim's downfall.

Wilder also chose a young has-been to play the gigolo. William Holden had been a young lead with a promising future before going off to war but had been relegated to B movies since returning from the front.

So the role-playing was there not only in the screenplay, but was also reflected in reality. And this reality was that of cinema — a dream factory, a lie peddling more illusions than truth, a graveyard of ghosts not yet all dead. This is why *Sunset Boulevard* is a despairing film that ends with one last lie, in which a mad, murderous old star is made to believe that she is shooting a film so that she can be taken away to prison or an asylum.

Never had the perversion of cinema been attacked so fiercely; yet the film professionals chose to turn this indictment into a triumph (giving it an Oscar for Best Film) rather than acknowledging

Gloria Swanson and Buster Keaton on the set of *Sunset Boulevard* (1950).

The final scene of *Sunset Boulevard*

Wilder rarely employs formal virtuosity. His apparently neutral style masks the subtlety of his *mise-en-scène*. It's only in moments of death or madness that he moves away from this principle. The end of *Sunset Boulevard* exemplifies this. It is designed as the (fake) realization of Norma Desmond's dream of standing once more before the cameras; she doesn't realize that her crime means her request will be granted, but in a different way.

The man who had first discovered and married her and then became her servant joins forces with the doctors and police to get her to leave the house. He tells her she's going to shoot her great scene, descending the grand staircase, and thus transforms the newsreel cameras into film cameras. He then 'directs' Norma in her last moments of normality, closing the parenthesis around the career he launched, so that we watch her pass from reality to illusion, from life to a legend tarnished by murder. They all surround her as the sad scene plays out. Norma walks round them, so she can be filmed, and becomes a moth guided by the dazzling spotlights. The series of shots reveals not just the woman's madness but also her crystallization as a ghost of cinema. And she becomes cinema, hears the music of the Salome she wanted DeMille to shoot for her screen comeback, then forgets everything around her to walk towards the camera, into the camera, turning herself into a blurred image for all, a phantom beyond time and representation.

Gloria Swanson and Erich von Stroheim in *Sunset Boulevard* (1950).

Following pages: Erich von Stroheim, William Holden and Gloria Swanson in *Sunset Boulevard* (1950).

their own guilt for the fall of all the industry's Norma Desmonds. Only Louis B. Mayer took offence, and Wilder publicly told him to get lost.

Portraits of scumbags

Wilder's success led his brother Wilhelm to quit his business in New York and move to Hollywood, where he produced and directed sixteen B movies devoid of importance or talent. Billy regretted this unsuccessful imitation by the only surviving member of his family, but did not get involved. He had recently married Audrey Young and split from Charles Brackett, with whom he no longer saw eye to eye, to go his own way. He produced several of his own films and changed screenwriters regularly until 1958.

Wilder launched this new period with *Ace in the Hole* (1951), a scathing parable about the public's fascination with morbid subjects and the way that journalists exploit it. (The title was later changed to *The Big Carnival*.) He made great use of his experience of the press in this portrait of a cynical, manipulative and ambitious social climber. Once again, Wilder's concept was at odds with the fashion, which was for portrayals of brave journalists who fought corruption and sought out the truth, as seen in film noir and melodramas. Wilder did not accept this shining image of the brave reporter and superimposed his own darker vision of Charles Tatum, an ambitious cheat who plays with the life and emotions of a man buried beneath a mountain by a collapsing cave. Tatum will do anything to get himself hired by a newspaper: he stages events and exploits the greed of the trapped man's wife to help him in his plans, strikes up an alliance with a corrupt sheriff and makes himself look like a hero in the eyes of the people who have flocked to the site of the story hoping to see the poor man's rescue or, more secretly, his death.

For the first and only time in his career, Wilder adopts a demonstrative style. His realism is even rather lumbering in some sequences. The director who was so wary of any appearance of virtuosity and always sought to maintain a concealed distance in his films experiments here with formal devices that are contrary to his usual clinical style. But they do not harm the quality of the whole, which is the film of an angry man.

In choosing the sneering Kirk Douglas to play Charles Tatum, he heightens the film's caustic Expressionism. At that time Douglas was often cast as a nasty cynic, and this time Wilder did not make him play against type, as he had with Fred MacMurray and Ray Milland. The aim of the film is to give this figure force, while also giving him enough humanity to avoid turning him into an over-simplified Manichaean caricature. The same process is at work in the portrayal of the other characters and of the crowd that gathers outside the mausoleum of a stranger made famous through the perversity of an ambitious journalist. But this complexity had its consequences. Furious at seeing themselves depicted as they truly behave in such circumstances, audiences stayed away. The film was Wilder's first flop, although the screenplay was nominated for an Oscar.

Sincerity didn't blunt his cunning. He sprang back with *Stalag 17* (1953), an adaptation of a successful stage play set in a World War II prisoner-of-war camp. War films were flourishing in Hollywood during the first half of the 1950s, but they were generally depictions of heroism or screwball comedies;

they never focused on the lives of prisoners of war. So Wilder's choice was unusual. He remembered Renoir's *Grand Illusion* (1937) and felt that something could be made of the subject. The comparison between the two films ends there, because *Stalag 17* is an acidic fable dominated by yet another portrait of a scumbag.

As in some of Wilder's earlier films, the story is told in voice-over. Here the narrator is a secondary character, 'employed' by Sefton, the main character played by William Holden. Sefton is a prisoner who traffics and schemes to get every advantage he can out of the situation. His fellow captives loathe him, but they all use him to access the black market and the entertainments he organizes to make money. When they find out there is a traitor in their hut, their suspicions are aroused, obliging Sefton to unmask the spy himself, not out of solidarity or patriotism, but to save his own skin.

The film begins and ends with an escape. The rest unfolds in the enclosed space of the camp, which becomes a theatre. *Stalag 17* is a meditation on performance, since everyone is playing a part to enable them to dream, dominate or spy on the

Kirk Douglas and Jan Sterling in *Ace in the Hole* (1951).

others. So the camp commandant, played by film director Otto Preminger, dons his boots to telephone his superiors; one of the prisoners wears a wig to cheer up his friend, who dreams of Betty Grable; an actor imitates the stars and stages a performance where everyone looks like Hitler; the spy turns out to be an irreproachably keen patriot.

Wilder's direction plays with the devices of theatre, even using insistent close-ups to create a disturbing distance, and farcical gags to break the suspense (a guard hands his gun to a prisoner so he can join in a game of volleyball). Here the realism lies not in the depiction of the way individuals behave, but in the expression of their fantasies, such as escape, or the belief that Sefton is the traitor.

Then everything is turned upside down by a line of dialogue, as social origins come to the fore with the arrival of a new prisoner from a rich background. This is the only point where Sefton talks about himself, saying he hadn't been able to go to West Point because his family was too poor. These words in no way justify his greedy individualism, but ultimately acquire their full weight when he escapes with the rich officer so he can make money out of him.

The film doesn't alternate moments of tragedy and comedy; as the iconic mask of Greek theatre suggests, the two combine, hence the near-absurd ambiguity that undermines the notions of compassion, loyalty and bravery the characters talk about. The grotesque and the tragic combine. The unmasked spy is thrown out into the night with saucepans tied to his ankles, a totally unlikely escape attempt that is nevertheless taken at face value by the guards, who shoot him dead. At this level of farce and play the implausible becomes magnificent. Lastly, and most subversively of all, the traitor is a German spy, in other words a patriot doing his duty, whereas Sefton enables the rich man's son to escape only to serve his own interests. Brave or not, a scumbag remains a scumbag — it's what makes him human after all. Wilder did not forget this later in creating the main characters of his scathing farces *The Apartment* (1960), *One, Two, Three* (1961) and *The Fortune Cookie* (1966).

Variations on the realization of a dream

Stalag 17 was a hit. William Holden won an Oscar. Wilder was back on top and returned to comedy with

Robert Strauss and Harvey Lembeck in *Stalag 17* (1953).

Personal stories

Gloria Swanson, actress
[On shooting *Sunset Boulevard*]
Billy Wilder deliberately left us on our own, made us dig into ourselves, knowing well that such a script, about Hollywood's excesses and neuroses, was bound to give the Hollywood people acting in it healthy doubts, about the material or about themselves, depending on their individual security. The more you thought about the film, the more it seemed to be a modern extension of Pirandello, or some sort of living exercise in science fiction. Early in the shooting, Bill Holden said that he needed to know more about Gillis in order to fill out the character, that the script was incomplete and unclear and therefore frustrating for him as an actor. 'How much do you know about Holden?' was all Billy Wilder would say.

This is an extract from Gloria Swanson, *Swanson on Swanson*, Random House, New York, 1980, pp. 481–2.

Marlene Dietrich, actress
He often used to say, 'I've got more than one trick up my sleeve.' He was a writer and director who was never short of resources and he loved the kind of challenges that made him improve on what he'd done before. Billy Wilder was like a master craftsman who knows his tools and uses them well to create a structure he can garland with his humour and wisdom.

This is an extract from Marlene Dietrich, *Marlene D.*, Grasset, Paris, 1984.

Miklos Rozsa, composer
Once a year I used to meet Billy Wilder at a Christmas party given by a mutual friend, the screenwriter Walter Reisch. At the party in 1971 he told me that he was going to make a picture about Sherlock Holmes, and that as Holmes was a violinist, he was going to use my Concerto. [...] I enjoyed adapting my Concerto. The first theme of the first movement was used for Holmes's cocaine addiction, the second movement for the love theme; the turbulent last movement became Loch Ness monster-music. For the scenes shot in the lovely Scottish highlands Wilder wanted Scottish music of some kind. As usual, I did my homework and wrote music based on some Scottish national tunes I had researched. Wilder complained it was too Scottish. The scene itself was a happy one, with Holmes, Watson and the 'Belgian' girl scooting along on bicycles. Then Wilder, perhaps remembering 'Bicycle Built For Two', asked for a waltz, but when he heard it he complained that it was too Viennese. There was only one session left, in two days' time, and he at last allowed me to write something that I considered appropriate. I used the love theme, but with an urgent, pulsating rhythm underneath, and it worked well.

This is an extract from Miklos Rozsa, *Double Life*, Wynwood Press, New York, 1982, pp. 194–5.

Samuel Fuller, director
Mankiewicz, Ben Hecht and Wilder are the three finest scriptwriters in the world. And Mankiewicz and Wilder are the best writer-directors. As an example of Billy's humour, Fellini was invited to Hollywood by the Directors Guild. There was a screening of *Satyricon*, followed by a discussion between directors. I was asked if I would be on the stage. They'd chosen two people, Billy and me. So we had the discussion, I said nothing – I had nothing to say. Nor did Billy. When it was over all the people came up to speak to Fellini. Billy walked over to me and said, 'Sam, I agree with everything you said.'

This is an extract from Samuel Fuller, Noël Simsolo and Jean Narboni, *Il était une fois Samuel Fuller*, Cahiers du cinéma, Paris, 1986.

an adaptation of *Sabrina*, a play by Samuel Taylor. The female lead was the young Audrey Hepburn, who had also just won an Oscar for her first Hollywood role in William Wyler's *Roman Holiday* (1953). So Paramount was ready to be generous, particularly as she was playing opposite William Holden. Once again, Wilder wanted Cary Grant to complete the cast, but he refused, and was replaced without enthusiasm by Humphrey Bogart. Wilder and Bogart did not get on, but that doesn't come through in the film. Like *The Emperor Waltz*, *Sabrina* (1954) takes the form of a fairy tale. A chauffeur's pretty daughter is in love with the boss's son David, an idle playboy. Despite the class difference she longs to marry him and is about to succeed when David's brother Linus decides to seduce her to prevent a union he sees as harmful to the family's interest. But Linus is caught in his own trap, falls for *Sabrina* and sails away with her to another dream called Paris.

Wilder was venturing into Cukor territory here and adopted a sophisticated *mise-en-scène* that breaks with his usual comedy style. Yet the meaning is no different from his previous films: *Sabrina*'s

Marcel Dalio (right) and Audrey Hepburn in *Sabrina* (1954).

obsession makes her socially ambitious. Her desperate desire to have her dream come true leads her subversively into a world of lies, compromise and manipulation, where everyone's behaviour is base and there's more bitterness than gentleness. When the film was released in Paris, Jacques Doniol-Valcroze pertinently highlighted its serious nature in his article 'Les métamorphoses cruelles' [Cruel transformations]: '*Sabrina* is reminiscent of Molière's *School for Wives* and Wilder is as tough with Arnolphe as with Agnès. He's tough on the puppets of the salon and the woman who longs to enter it, but also on the kitchen staff: Sabrina's father lets things happen — he's embarrassed and reticent, but cowardly. Meanwhile the other servants act as Sabrina's sycophantic accomplices and voyeurs to boot (see the ballroom scene and the rather odious sign of understanding that passes between them and Sabrina — how to get the boss's son to marry you). Ultimately he is indulgent only towards David, a rather simple womanizer whose heart is nevertheless pure and who sacrifices himself a burnt offering to the plastics cartel and the rejuvenation of his bad brother.'[11]

43

William Holden, Audrey Hepburn and Humphrey Bogart in *Sabrina* (1954).

Tom Ewell and Marilyn Monroe
in *The Seven Year Itch* (1955).

Opposite page: Marilyn Monroe in *The Seven Year Itch* (1955).

Following pages: Marilyn Monroe
and Tom Ewell in *The Seven Year Itch* (1955).

Wilder followed *Sabrina* with a commission from Fox, to which Paramount had lent him. This was *The Seven Year Itch* (1955), adapted from a successful play by George Axelrod and famous for its female lead, Marilyn Monroe, and the subway ventilator scene where her dress blows up to reveal her thighs.

But the film — the story of a married man left on his own one summer in New York, who meets a pretty blonde — didn't please Wilder. Censorship stopped him showing adultery and he was also unable to impose his choice of new face Walter Matthau in the main role. Obliged to accept Tom Ewell, who had played the role in the play and takes the film in the direction of vaudeville, Wilder adds farcical and cynical touches to go beyond the stereotypes and sugar of the script, subtly superimposing mental images on part of the CinemaScope screen. He also manages to give frank expression to the sexual urges of his main character through the presence of Monroe, whose animal sensuality sucks up the lifeblood of the film. Years later Wilder would show what *The Seven Year Itch* might have been with a few explicit sequences in *Kiss Me, Stupid*. Working with Monroe proved exhausting. Everyone on set was subjected to her caprices, but she is excellent in the film.

James Stewart in *The Spirit of St. Louis* (1957).

After disagreements with Paramount, Wilder left the studio and was no longer the producer of his films. The status of independent director was unusual in Hollywood at the time and few could survive that way, but Wilder had the luck to make hits that helped him retain his freedom. He shot *Spirit of St. Louis* (1957), a biopic of the pioneering transatlantic airman Charles Lindbergh, for Warner Bros. It was a film in a different register from those that had brought him glory. Lindbergh refused to allow it to be about anything other than his feat of aviation. Wilder accepted this limitation and worked on a screenplay with a fragmented structure of flashbacks linked to Lindbergh's obsession with flying across the Atlantic. Like all of his generation, Wilder had been marked by the event. This empirical aspect is a handicap he overcomes by using distance dilated in counterpoint by the film score written by his friend Franz Waxman and the eloquent eyes of actor James Stewart. Unable to set out his favourite themes here, he orchestrates the whole around the theme of obstinacy, with a concern for realistic behaviour that rules out heroism and spectacular effects. So Lindbergh talks to a fly caught in the pilot's cabin; he is awoken from dangerous sleep by a ray of sunlight; he melts the ice weighing down his wings by changing altitude. All these things have a documentary air and this was what Lindbergh wanted. He read the screenplay, ready to stop everything if it did not respect his immaculate image. He was a tough man with very reactionary views. Yet Wilder ventured to tease him:

'One day when we were flying to Washington, Charles Lindbergh and I, we were going to the Smithsonian Institution to see the real *Spirit of St. Louis*, which we had duplicated. Hanging off the ceiling, it's there. And we were in a plane flying to Washington, and it's very very rough, so I turned to him and I said, "Charles, wouldn't that be fun if this plane now crashed, can you see the headlines?— Lucky Lindy in crash with Jewish friend!" And he said, "Oh, no no no, don't talk like this!"'[12]

After this experience Wilder decided to produce and adapt *Ariane, jeune fille russe*, a novel by Claude Anet, which had been filmed by Paul Czinner in 1931, in a French-language version with Gaby Morlay, and in German and English versions with Elisabeth Bergner. He hired Audrey Hepburn and Cary Grant, but Grant backed out at the last minute and was replaced by Gary Cooper.

The story was transposed to contemporary Paris and Wilder decided to shoot it in the city that had seen his beginnings as a director. This enabled him to begin a long collaboration with the artistic director Alexandre Trauner, whom he had met on the set of *The Spirit of St. Louis* in Le Bourget airport.

Alexandre Trauner was a Jew of Hungarian origins who had been artistic director on Marcel Carné's films before the War and had continued to work clandestinely under the Occupation. After the Liberation he began an international career, designing Howard Hawks's *Land of the Pharaohs* (1955). He went on to make eight films with Wilder.

Love in the Afternoon (1957) was Wilder's first collaboration with I. A. L. Diamond, known as Izzy Diamond. Their adaptation is a bitter-sweet variation on obsession and desire. Starting from a comic premise — a private detective's daughter pretends to a past of promiscuity in order to attract a rich but ageing American Don Juan — Wilder uses ambiguity and shifts in tone, moving abruptly from gags to emotion, to create a film that is far more serious than funny. It does not contain the notion of transference that took *Sabrina* from the arms of a carefree playboy to those of an older businessman. Here both are combined in Gary Cooper's character, who is an echo of the millionaire of *Bluebeard's Eighth Wife*, the first filmscript Wilder wrote for Lubitsch. Another reference to Lubitsch can be seen in the presence of his favourite actor, Maurice Chevalier.

For Wilder, *Love in the Afternoon* summed up his preceding films and opened the way to a new period in his work. From that point on, the style and subjects of his films were parables whose improprieties were concealed in a deceptively simple form. This made their effect of realism all the more powerful, but for a while audiences were charmed by these exercises in target shooting without realizing that they were fables of moral disillusionment.

Love in the Afternoon is an apology for lying. A young virgin of humble origins persuades a modern Casanova that she engages in free love. This lie excites the libertine, who, on realizing he has been tricked, thinks the girl will change his life, not necessarily with her gentleness, but with her Scheherazade side, her ability to invent erotic adventures that will excite him by making him jealous. The happy ending at the station emerges from tears of distress because it is the product of a fool's game. Neither the spineless seducer nor the innocent liar has escaped the vice resulting from their respective obsessions. They have each become a prisoner of a dream susceptible to becoming a daily nightmare. Despite its comic moments, *Love in the Afternoon* is a tragedy.

Billy Wilder in conversation

You just have to have the pace of every scene of the film in your head. When I arrive on set I ask myself about the scene I'm going to shoot, why is it there, how is it paced. I hope the actors have studied their lines and I say to them, 'Off you go.' They begin and sometimes they bring something better than what I'd thought of. When that happens I use it. If they're bad I correct them, as calmly as possible, but I never give them a list of things to do. I don't tell them, 'Now you take out a cigarette, then you look this way, then that way, then you take a step over there.'... I want everyone on set to feel they are contributing. Actors like that. Some arrive on set totally empty. You have to tell them everything. Often they're very good actors. Then there are the ones who are very pretentious. You have to explain everything to them from the start, things like, your uncle was a pederast and long ago... etc., things that have nothing to do with the film and will never appear in it. But they really like that because they think good old Wilder has studied Freud and they're flattered. Others are stupid. With them you have to be direct and primitive. Actors are patients and we're the doctor who has to adapt to different clients. They're also like bridge partners, you have to understand how they play if you want to work as a team with them. You have to sense the way they see things. With an actor you have to think whether he's going to be embarrassed by this or that thought, this or that theme, whether or not he's capable of adding something, if he has the resources, the technique or the style to do it. Some actors can help you tell the story.

This is an extract from an interview with Billy Wilder by Jean Domarchi and Jean Douchet published in *Cahiers du cinéma*, 134 (August 1962).

Audrey Hepburn and Maurice Chevalier in *Love in the Afternoon* (1957).

Marlene Dietrich in *Witness for the Prosecution* (1957).

Intermezzo with living legends

In 1957 Marlene Dietrich was refusing most of the film roles she was offered, preferring to tour as a singer. But when she was offered *Witness for the Prosecution* (1957), adapted from a novel and play by Agatha Christie, she accepted on condition that Wilder directed. He agreed. The 'commission' suited him, with its themes of lying, inversion and role play, explored in the context of a thriller. He was also happy to be able to direct Charles Laughton[13] in the role of an important lawyer fooled by his client. 'I told you that when we had a big scene coming up the next day, Laughton would come to my room, and he would do that big scene, and know every word. Then he would do it differently. Then he would do it another way, twenty times. And he was better and better and better. [...] I just had to choose. [...] We had rehearsed in the day before, and by then were kind of happy with version number twenty, let's say. Then he came to the studio the next morning, and said he had an entirely different idea of working up to the big line "...Or are you not a LIAR?!" He had the idea of staying quiet, working up to it. So we did it, we kind of combined twenty and twenty-one. The whole thing we did in one close-up. You could see the whole up-and-down, the scale of the actor...'[14]

Witness for the Prosecution is a film in which all the actors have to speak and express themselves in a range of different ways according to the profession, physical position, duality, disguise and psychology of their characters, who are all entangled in big or small lies.

Marlene Dietrich and Tyrone Power take part in this exercise of theatrical lying structured around sudden changes of circumstance. The tragedy and comedy are played out in the closed spaces of a lawyer's office, a courtroom and a station buffet. The unease underlying the trial is heightened by two flashbacks. First we go to Dietrich's Berlin cabaret act in a defeated Germany — a reference to *A Foreign Affair* — where she seems to marry the first man who comes along in order to make a new life. Then Tyrone Power's encounters with the widow invert the situation of the German scenes, with the man playing the gigolo in the hope that this rich woman will lift him out of poverty.

Above and beyond the pretext of a murder motivated by money, this is a sordid world. The plot is strong and the Hitchcock-style suspense perfectly constructed. The director's inventions work perfectly and Agatha Christie was pleased with this film, through which Wilder's world emerges in fragmented fashion.

Charles Laughton, John Williams and Marlene Dietrich in *Witness for the Prosecution* (1957).

Following pages:
Left: Audrey Hepburn and Gary Cooper in *Love in the Afternoon* (1957).
Right: Humphrey Bogart and Audrey Hepburn in *Sabrina* (1954).

Jack Lemmon, Tony Curtis and Marilyn Monroe
in *Some Like It Hot* (1959).

Wo(men)

The collaboration between Diamond and Wilder led
to international success with *Some Like It Hot* (1959),
the first film Wilder made for the Mirisch Company,
which became his financial partner for his next
seven films. It was also the start of his collaboration with the actor Jack Lemmon and his second
film with Marilyn Monroe.

    The basic plot — men dress up as women to
work in an all-woman orchestra — was taken from
a film by Kurt Hoffmann, *Fanfaren des Liebe* (1951),
itself a German remake of a French film, *Fanfare
d'amour*, directed by Richard Pottier in 1935.

    At a time when the film industry was churn-
ing out colour blockbusters in an effort to overcome
the competition from television, Wilder opted for
black and white. He also decided to combine the
gangster genre with farce and to play the retro
card by setting his story in the 1920s. Everyone
said the film would flop, but everyone was wrong.
It was a triumph.

    Wilder's stroke of genius was to parody the
old-style gangster and comedy-chase genres, but
turn them upside down to make them subversive
and crazy. As an *auteur* who often used inversion,
this film offered a perfect opportunity to take that
process to radical extremes.

    First there are the characters. The vampish
singer Sugar turns into a naive girl who falls prey
to her own illusions. The attractive millionaire is
a dirty old man with an infantile streak. The gangsters act like bourgeois and their boss, George Raft,
acts like a novice who keeps falling victim to scams.

    The process unfolds in several different ways
through the two musicians, who first turn into
women, then become so entangled in their roles
that they lose their grip on their own identities. The
saxophonist, the masculine half of the pair logically
played by the virile Tony Curtis, is the 'confidante'
of Sugar — Marilyn — to whom he is attracted. A
bellboy makes a pass at him and he doesn't know
how to get rid of him. Donning a male disguise to
seduce Sugar, he pretends to be a handsome, impotent millionaire (with the voice of Cary Grant!), but
cannot maintain one aspect of this role when faced

Jack Lemmon and Marilyn Monroe in *Some Like It Hot* (1959).

Triumphant comedy

Billy Wilder brought a new tone to American comedy. He knew how to make audiences laugh and alternated hilarious dialogue with comic situations that often verged on slapstick. His fondness for cross-dressing and sexual misunderstandings no doubt stemmed from his time frequenting the Berlin cabarets of the Weimar Republic. Lubitsch, one of his mentors, had received the same influence, but erased its crude and vulgar aspects from his American films. Conversely he was able to retain the ambiguities that gave it all its savour and distilled it brilliantly.

Working with Lubitsch, Wilder learned to refine his comic effects by pacing and structuring them. But he still added plenty of social critique. His comedies became farces as much as satires. Lying and dressing up were his favouring means of making audiences laugh. He also used the inversion, as opposed to reversal, of situations. His characters are constantly having to change identity or sex to get themselves out of trouble. And being stubborn about it, they get caught up in their own schemes and sink into paranoia or schizophrenia.

Great comic creators characteristically proceed in this way. From Molière to Sacha Guitry, Charlie Chaplin to Jerry Lewis, these geniuses have amused the public with techniques of this kind. In that respect Wilder is a classic *auteur*.

Marilyn Monroe, Jack Lemmon and Tony Curtis in *Some Like It Hot* (1959).

with Sugar's sexual persuasion (Oh, Marilyn!) and loses his identity in shifting from one role to the next. He gets it back only when he reveals that he is a man disguised as a woman, first publicly kissing the singer — in visual terms this is two women kissing — then taking off his wig, showing Sugar that he is a fake millionaire, but also revealing himself to the gangsters as the troublesome witness to the St Valentine's Day massacre.

The double bass player, an eternally feather-brained Jack Lemmon, is the feminine side of the duo, so he benefits from only a single system of inversion — his disguise as a woman, which he maintains throughout the film. Courted by an old (and genuine) millionaire, he carries his second identity through to the limit, allowing himself to be wined and dined, dancing a tango with a rose in his teeth and accepting expensive gifts, and only admits he is a man after making several other excuses to turn down the offer of marriage. When he confesses, 'I'm a man' and takes off his wig, while retaining his make-up and earrings, his suitor makes the priceless reply, 'Nobody's perfect'. The absolute absurdity of the situation prevents him from regaining his identity. Whatever he does, he remains a betrothed in disguise.

Wilder orchestrates all this using the same system, substituting one disguise for another. From alternating curtains in the overnight train to the bubble bath hiding the sailor's uniform, women playing hot jazz, characters with no overcoats in mid-winter, the faking of a funeral as a means of getting drunk and murderous gangsters singing 'For he's a jolly good fellow', everything is a matter of masks and feedback.

The secondary gags follow the same principle: the bass player spins his instrument as he stares at Sugar's body and starts playing the back, where there are no strings.

Wilder remains true to his themes in this orgy of comedy where the sexual allusions become so inflated that they suppress the vulgarity of the subject. Here again are relationships between people from different worlds and differentiated sexes, cynical greed, lies and imposture. Except that the saxophonist stops being a scumbag and is finally sincere with Sugar when the masks are dropped. But the pessimistic Wilder isn't used to happy endings and knocks this one off-kilter by highlighting the other couple formed by the bass player and the real millionaire. The farce ends with an absurd exchange that turns the film into a nightmare so grotesque that the American censors and the self-censorship of the audience can no longer reject its healthy obscenity. It is high art — a true masterpiece of burlesque comedy.

The final scene
of *Some Like It Hot*

Two romances, one between Tony Curtis and Marilyn Monroe, the other between Jack Lemmon and the millionaire, are compromised by cross-dressing. The comic potential of this situation is explored until the last scene, in which Tony Curtis reveals he is really a man. We see him sitting with Marilyn on the back seat of the boat, with Lemmon and the millionaire in the front. Wilder keeps the camera static and bases his *mise-en-scène* on the dialogue.

Lemmon's arguments are all rejected by his 'fiancé'. In the end he takes off his wig and announces that he's a man. The revelation makes no difference. The millionaire still wants to marry Lemmon.

In both cases, the abandonment of cross-dressing leads to the formation of a couple and reveals the underlying nature of each. Lemmon really was the feminine half of the couple he formed with Curtis. While 'nobody's perfect', it looks as though 'nobody's fooled' either, starting with the millionaire.

Top: Marilyn Monroe and Tony Curtis in *Some Like It Hot* (1959).

Bottom: Joe E. Brown and Jack Lemmon in *Some Like It Hot* (1959).

Opposite page: Jack Lemmon on the set of *Some Like It Hot* (1959).

Jack Lemmon in *The Apartment* (1960).

The return of Verism

Wilder once again suffered the caprices of Marilyn Monroe on the set of *Some Like It Hot*. He ruled out the possibility of working with her again, quipping, 'I have discussed this with my doctor and my psychiatrist and they tell me I'm too old and too rich to go through this again.'

Conversely he had so enjoyed working with Jack Lemmon that he made him the star of his next film, *The Apartment* (1960), the story of an ambitious office worker who lends his apartment to his superiors so that they can commit discreet adultery. Wilder had got the idea fifteen years previously when he saw David Lean's *Brief Encounter* (1945), and now the relaxation of censorship made the film possible. He treats it as a comedy-drama and uses black

and white CinemaScope to obtain a realism in the Verist spirit that marked his work in Berlin.

The Apartment is a dark, disillusioned film in which everyone drinks, fornicates (except the main character) and passes themselves off as someone they are not in a series of enclosed physical and mental spaces, each more ugly than the last. The fantasy of personal social success is depicted as never before. A man may not himself sleep with someone in the hope of promotion, but he allows others to do so with the same aim — the sordidness of this world is far murkier than that oozing from satires and melodramas dealing with similar subjects.

Once again, the film abounds in inversions. The office worker's energy is channelled into allocating the use of his apartment between his

Jack Lemmon and Shirley MacLaine in *The Apartment* (1960).

Following pages: Jack Lemmon (centre) in *The Apartment* (1960).

various superiors rather than into his work. His neighbours think he's a party animal when in fact he lives alone with no sex life at all. His boss gives him a promotion instead of firing him for his schemes and even asks if he can use the premises himself. This is all a sad reflection of an everyday reality of lies and manipulation in which frustration is compensated by adultery. And to achieve this, everyone exploits the power of their own class: executives provide alcohol, the boss gives his mistress money for Christmas. It's a world of vampires where everyone selfishly pursues his or her own pleasures and desires.

Yet the lonely, ambitious office worker is also a romantic. He loves the lift attendant who is his boss's mistress and finds out the truth too late not to be hurt. When he achieves the success he coveted, he lets it all go, sickened by himself and others, and becomes the *mensch* (human being) his doctor neighbour talks about. He then gets the girl he loves, who has dumped the boss. Wilder said this proves that he had not (for once) made a pessimistic film. But the characters playing rummy at the end are both unemployed. They have lost their illusions by refusing to compromise and have moved to the margins of society, since those who refuse to play the game lose all hope of social success.

By a typically American paradox, this film that so implacably criticizes the country's institutions was rewarded with a shedload of Oscars, three of which went to Wilder: Best Director, Best Picture and Best Screenplay.

Billy Wilder, by Jean Douchet

And then there's Billy Wilder's taste.

We have to admit it's pretty bad, very turn-of-the-century Viennese baroque, spiced up with a personal penchant for sleazy situations and disgusting sights. It takes a love of the morbid to try to touch people – even without also making them laugh – with more than half an hour of medical care given to a woman who has attempted suicide. This ugliness can be seen at every level of the *mise-en-scène*. The cinematography is full of blacks, the sets are gloomy and oppressive, and the actors' performances are at once allusive and emphatic, in the tradition of Lubitsch, without his grace and vivacity. All in all, it's an updated version of 1925 Expressionism.

Yet despite these faults, the style is there, and it expresses a highly coherent vision of the world. For Wilder, human beings are wading in mire. Their cowardice makes their position almost hopeless. Salvation can come only if they acknowledge their state. Profound disgust gives rise to a nostalgia for purity. Ultimately, Wilder's characters are romantics, idealists sunk in depravity, which is itself a consequence of the decadence of a civilization, the decay of a society. He bases his direction of actors on grimaces. This is not for reasons of convenience. They express a fundamental disquiet, a moral repulsion and secret suffering at the abasement imposed on them by social structures that flout the most elementary laws of human dignity.

This is an extract from 'L'École de Vienne (*The Apartment*)', Cahiers du cinéma, 113 (November 1960).

Billy Wilder on the set of *One, Two, Three* (1961).

Opposite page: Pamela Tiffin (standing) and Horst Buchholtz (centre) in *One, Two, Three* (1961).

The great manipulator

Anti-communism is a recurrent theme in Wilder's films. He had never been fascinated by the Soviet model, and this rejection can be seen as far back as his work on Lubitsch's *Ninotchka*. For Wilder, any country governed by one party is a dictatorship. Despite his furious individualism, he never denounced anyone during the witch-hunts, but he did allow himself a bad joke about the Hollywood Ten, who were condemned as 'unfriendly witnesses' for refusing to appear before the Committee on Un-American Activities: 'Of the ten, two had talent and the rest were just unfriendly.'

And when he made the staccato-paced *One, Two, Three* (1961), a broad farce set in the Berlin of 1960, his jibes at the Soviet Union were so fierce that he was reproached by left-wing critics.

Diamond and Wilder took a play by Ferenc Molnár[15] as their starting point for a screenplay that does not confine itself to satirizing the USSR.

The USA comes in for its fair share too. The head of Coca-Cola in Germany wants to move into the Soviet market. He is also playing host to his boss's daughter, who falls in love with a communist, marries him and becomes pregnant. To save his own job, the businessman turns this young man into an ardent capitalist.

The film has a burlesque power beyond any ideological critique. It is stuffed full of visual gags, from a portrait of Stalin hidden under that of Khrushchev to the Soviet car that falls to pieces like something out of a Laurel and Hardy movie. The direction is brilliant and effective. James Cagney brings his own sense of timing to the frantic manipulation, which, as always with Wilder, unfolds in subtle variations on inversion and disguise. The Soviet police torture a suspected spy by making him listen to a stupid American novelty song and James Cagney gives the young communist a new identity by means of high-speed brainwashing, managing

Peter Capell, Leon Askin, Liselotte Pulver, James Cagney and Ralf Wolter in *One, Two, Three* (1961).

Hans Lothar, James Cagney, Horst Buchholtz and Pamela Tiffin in *One, Two, Three* (1961).

to make him even more capitalist and ambitious than he is himself. Thus it becomes clear that the Americans are far more effective than the Soviets when it comes to colonizing minds.

So Wilder spares no one and enjoys irritating everyone by showing how everything can be bought and corrupted; but he never forgets that capitalism eats itself through competition (the gag of the drinks machine that gives out Pepsi instead of Coca-Cola).

But *One, Two, Three* fell foul of events. It was released while the Berlin wall was being built and the public didn't feel like laughing about the Cold War. It was Wilder's first commercial flop since *Ace in the Hole*.

Prostitution of all kinds

All Wilder's films deal more or less with prostitution, but, due to censorship or the setting of the screenplay, he had not depicted any actual prostitutes apart from one bar hostess character in *The Lost Weekend*. With *Irma la Douce* (1963), he placed a prostitute at the centre of the film and made a spectacular return to box-office success. Wilder and Diamond took the film's structure from the original French musical of the same name, leaving out the songs and adding gags, secondary characters and louche situations in which bad taste is paradoxically combined with a great stylistic elegance heightened by Trauner's sets and colour, drawing on pre-war poetic realism.

Lou Jacobi and Jack Lemmon in *Irma la Douce* (1963).

Wilder again used his favourite actor Jack Lemmon and refused to give the role of Irma to Brigitte Bardot, who wanted it, preferring Shirley MacLaine, with whom he had enjoyed working in *The Apartment*.

The burlesque style and the coded colour-fulness of the Paris underworld do not reduce this film to a grotesque farce. Realism is always present behind the masks and clichés, since the plot's twists and turns depend on the emotions of the charac-ters in this fable about love, sex and money set in the closed world of the food market of Les Halles.

The credit sequence reveals a neighbour-hood that lives by the consumption of food and women, with both categories of merchandise on display. The latter use appearance, dress and make-up to whet their clients' appetites, even adopting the latest fashion by trying to look like Nabakov's Lolita as seen in Stanley Kubrick's film. So Wilder establishes dressing up as a driver of his fiction. From Irma's green stockings to her pimp's painted English lord, all fantasies converge in a moment of truth when — rare event in Wilder's films — a child is born.

The astounding thing is that the stereotypes cancel each other out in a loop effect that saps energy and does away with trivial functions. This story of a former policeman turned unwilling pimp, adopting the disguise of her single, rich, impotent client so that his protégée will sleep with no one but him, is a fairy tale in which sordidness is transformed into tenderness. While the character of Irma is monolithic, Jack Lemmon's has to become a quick-change artist to preserve his underlying identity. And as everything has to be paid for — money is the other subject of the film — he secretly works in the market at Les Halles so he can hand over large sums to the woman he loves when he visits her at night under another identity. But he also has to preserve his appearance as a pimp to keep hold of a prostitute who takes a professional pride in her work. His position is so schizophrenic that he murders the lord he has invented so he can stop being jealous of himself. But then he looks like a real murderer.

This completes Wilder's exposition. His film now dives into the absurd to avoid slipping into traditional morality, while implausibility makes it possible to reveal the tenderness he feels for this truly loving couple. *Irma la Douce* is perhaps Wilder's only optimistic film.

Billy Wilder and Shirley MacLaine on the set of *Irma la Douce* (1963).

Opposite page: Shirley MacLaine in *Irma la Douce* (1963).

Following pages: Jack Lemmon and Shirley MacLaine in *Irma la Douce* (1963).

Kim Novak, Ray Walston and Dean Martin in *Kiss Me, Stupid* (1964).

The art of screenplay writing

Wilder started out in the cinema as a screenplay writer and, as the years went by, assimilated the advice of two masters of the art, Carl Mayer and Ernst Lubitsch. But he always worked with a co-writer, first Charles Brackett, a man in every way different from him in life, but capable of setting up a productive dialogue in creating scripts. Over the years that they worked together, they brought realism to traditional comedy and drama with equal success. However, Brackett's social background and reactionary attitudes led Wilder to decide against working with him on *Double Indemnity* and to hire Raymond Chandler, who brought undeniable originality to the dialogue.

Later Wilder stopped working with Brackett and hired other scriptwriters, before meeting I. A. L. Diamond, with whom he afterwards worked continuously. He described their working method to Jean Domarchi and Jean Douchet as follows: 'Sometimes we write, sometimes we talk. When we're in despair we shut up. Sometimes we write twelve pages in an afternoon. Anything can happen. We stay in my room from 9 am to 6 pm, as regular as office workers. The hard thing isn't pulling ideas out of nowhere, it's starting with millions of ideas, most of which bear no relation to what we're doing. The first big job is to throw out everything you don't need.' (Cahiers du cinéma, 134, August 1962). First of all Wilder is

looking for things that will have an unstoppable effect on the audience, without being flashy. On his office wall is a revealing sign that says, 'What would Lubitsch have done?'
It is interesting to note that the two writers got stuck on the last scene of *Some Like It Hot*. Diamond had suggested the line 'Nobody's perfect', which they put in the middle of the sequence. As nothing came to them that would do as the last word, they moved the line to the end temporarily, hoping to find something better before the scene was shot. Having failed to do so, they kept it out of bafflement and were astounded to observe its extraordinary comic impact on audiences. Wilder never believed in improvising

a scene on set. His screenplay was not the architecture of the film to come, but the whole film. The direction was just its orchestration in the light of the tempos of the actors and the cadence of the whole. Sets, scores and editing were dependent on this written basis, and the specifics of filming alone could justify the inclusion of new ideas for dialogue and situations. But this absolute control was not enough to ensure Wilder achieved the effects he was after, as he had known since he started out as a director. He noted the unnecessary nature of the final scenes of *Double Indemnity* and his strategic error in the morgue opening of *Sunset Boulevard*, afterwards avoiding any redundant scenes or discrepancies of tone.

Billy Wilder with Kim Novak on the set of *Kiss Me, Stupid* (1964).

Dean Martin and Kim Novak in *Kiss Me, Stupid* (1964).

Prostitution is also the theme of the film that follows, a very free adaptation of Anna Bonacci's play *L'Ora della fantasia* entitled *Kiss Me, Stupid* (1964).

The story tells of two provincials who write songs and dream of selling them. Chance brings Las Vegas singing star Dino their way, and they keep him in town to try and reach their goal, paying a prostitute to play one of their wives and go with the singer so she can persuade him to put one of their songs into his show. But a series of reversals and misunderstandings lead Dino to sleep with the musician's real wife rather than the prostitute.

American comedy was flourishing in this period. Blake Edwards had just made his name with *The Pink Panther* (1963), in which the actor Peter Sellers earned star status and, as Jack Lemmon wasn't available, Wilder hired Sellers for *Kiss Me, Stupid*. But Sellers did not accept his director's

instructions and the atmosphere at the start of filming was very tense. When Sellers had a heart attack, Wilder could replace him with Ray Walston, who had played a supporting role in *The Apartment*.

The other male lead was offered to Dean Martin, who had enough of a sense of humour to agree to play a caricatured version of his own image. The cast was completed by Kim Novak and Felicia Farr, otherwise known as Mrs Jack Lemmon.

Kiss Me, Stupid shows that all dreams can come true for those who are prepared to cynically pay the price. The two songwriters see their song sung by Dino on his television show. The wife of one of them lives out her teenage fantasy by sleeping with the singer, who thinks she's a prostitute. Dino unwittingly makes love with the wife promised him by the husband. Polly, the prostitute, has two wishes come true: first by spending a night as a 'married woman', and then by receiving the money Dino had given to the woman she has replaced, and who replaced her, enabling her to buy a car and leave town.

This is a fool's game where everyone wins. It was precisely for that reason that morality campaigners criticized and attacked it. Wilder was surprised. He saw *Kiss Me, Stupid* as a chaste, decent film. But it does pack a punch, even though it pursues his perennial theme of the revelation of reality through dressing up and role play. There can be no fantasies without underlying desire; so states the law of ambivalence, and Wilder's film offers the most persuasive proof of this. Whatever they may say, the jealous man is excited by the idea that his wife is unfaithful, the married woman by the idea of being a whore, the prostitute by the idea of living a moral life, and the seducer by that of paying for his pleasure. These unconscious motives foster a shift from comedy to drama. The 'nobody's perfect' principle remains the same.

The last film in the trilogy, *The Fortune Cookie* (1966), deals with the more underhand form of prostitution that is fraud. A television cameraman is hurt by a player during a football match. His brother-in-law gets him to pretend to be paralysed so he can claim compensation. His pretence unfairly destroys the falsely accused party, while drawing him in as a friend and unwitting servant of the odious scam. Here everyone is acting except the football player, who likes the man who is destroying him. It's no coincidence that Wilder chose a black actor to play the footballer, who becomes a servant in a voluntary act of submission. In the American society of his day, everyone had a place as long as they remained powerful or hidden, in the glare of publicity or buried in the shadows of mediocrity. As in *The Apartment*, the cameraman ultimately becomes a *mensch* and drives his victim to be a *mensch* once more by forcing him to play football with him in an empty stadium. But their future does not look promising. They will always remain victims.

In this film Wilder once again brought together Jack Lemmon and Walter Matthau, whose comic potential he had noted during the preparation of *The Seven Year Itch*. They made a great duo, which many other directors would reunite.

Jack Lemmon in *The Fortune Cookie* (1966).

The Last Sparks

From *The Private Life of Sherlock Holmes* to *Buddy Buddy*

Colin Blakely and Robert Stephens
in *The Private Life of Sherlock Holmes* (1970).

Mutilated masterpiece

To Wilder's surprise, *The Fortune Cookie* flopped, and he sensed that the audiences who had so enjoyed laughing at his crazy comic vision in *Some Like It Hot* and *Irma la Douce* disliked the darkness of his recent comedies. He hesitated between several subjects before settling on a colour film in CinemaScope that was never to be shown in its uncut version: *The Private Life of Sherlock Holmes* (1970).

He and Diamond invented several adventures focused on the private life of Conan Doyle's detective. They turned the legend upside down, showing the hero manipulated by others and with little aptitude for solving riddles. This reversal of the myth went hand in hand with a subtle game of appearances, whose spectacular aspect was confined to the formal perfection of each image, since there are no bravura elements in the detective story.

The mechanism can be illustrated by a short sequence: a terrified policeman takes refuge on a flight of steps, but this is merely to avoid getting his feet soaked by a municipal sprinkler. In this film heroism and strangeness are replaced by trivial realism: the Loch Ness monster is simply a camouflage for the trials of a submarine. So all is lies and illusion. One of the sections of the film that was cut illustrates this perfectly. Holmes was taken to a room where the furniture was stuck to the ceiling. This 'mystery of the upside-down room' proved to have been staged by Watson in order to stop his friend taking drugs.

The start of the film, showing the opening of Watson's secret papers in 1971, was cut from the final version, as was an initial episode with a train, made in a style more burlesque than mysterious. This is a shame, as the sequence showed how Watson embellished things by confusing a simple case of adultery with a mysterious crime.

However, what remains in the truncated version shows that the film's major theme is deception. All the clues interpreted by Holmes have been fabricated to lead him to where his enemies and allies want him to go. He is a victim of appearances and proves incapable of unmasking unassisted the female spy who has gained his confidence and, perhaps, his love.

Another sequence that was cut showed him returning from an investigation in a harem. On the boat he left his friend Watson to work out for him the mystery of the death of the young newly weds.

All in all, in this film the sleuth's gifts are used only for ends other than solving a mystery. 89

Meanwhile his sexuality was evoked in a third section cut from the film, a memory from his student days in which he discovered that the woman he was in love with was a prostitute.

The version released retains only a scene about the rumour of homosexuality between himself and Watson. Holmes uses this pretext to refuse the proposition of the Russian ballet master, who asks him to get the dancer pregnant in exchange for a Stradivarius. Watson falls victim to his friend's lies about their relationship.

But here too there is a cut. A scene showed the ballet master visiting Holmes the next day, bringing flowers and the violin. He asked the housekeeper for Mr and Mrs Holmes and gave the detective the violin, explaining that the composer Tchaikovsky had declined the same offer, but had received a grand piano. Then he gave Watson the flowers, discreetly suggesting an amorous tryst.

While these mutilations are unfortunate, the fact remains that *The Private Life of Sherlock Holmes* is still a magnificent film, even though it has lost some of Wilder's intentions. It is not so much a tragicomedy as a symphony, an impression accentuated by the music of Miklos Rozsa, based on his Violin Concerto, Opus 24, written for Jascha Heifetz in 1953.

The good life

Although he was associate producer of *The Private Life of Sherlock Holmes*, Wilder was unable to prevent parts of it being amputated as required by his partners. He realized that production methods had changed and regretted the mutations the industry had undergone since the explosion of the New Wave, most of which he rejected. Disconcerted by the situation, he pursued several projects but was unable to bring any of them to fruition.

In 1972 Wilder produced and directed a film less cynical than usual.

'Avanti! is a film of a kind that doesn't get made much nowadays, a romantic movie dealing with contemporary themes and which I have scrupulously tried not to make pretentious. It started out as a play by Samuel Taylor, whose *Sabrina* I'd already adapted. [...] I didn't use any of it, apart from the initial situation: an American man and an Englishwoman go to Italy to collect the bodies of their parents, his father and her mother, who have been killed in a car accident. He's a very prim, high-society American with right-wing views, who starts to look at his father and his own life in a different light. Thirty-six hours later he goes back to America a different man. It's a kind of coming-of-age story,

Geneviève Page and Robert Stephens in *The Private Life of Sherlock Holmes* (1970).

Opposite page: Jack Lemmon in *Avanti!* (1972).

treated lightly, without any pseudo-philosophizing, because in my mind I always have the idea that our first duty is to provide the audience with two and a half hours of relaxation, pleasure and laughter, with something to think about now and then, without shoving boring, sententious messages down their throats.'[16]

Whatever he may say, in *Avanti!* Wilder shows contemporary America and tourist traps in a harsh light. An American goes to Italy where his father has just died, and discovers he had a double life. Before opting for the same happy adultery as his father, he defends the system based on money and the paternalism of bosses, as indicated by his plan to broadcast the funeral to the factory workers on CCTV. His father's fidelity to both his mistress and his wife does not make him forget that he belonged to the dominant social class.

These things do not prevent true love and can lead to tenderness, but *Avanti!* is about power, from the hotel manager's scheming to the political and economic power of the son, played by Jack Lemmon. A US diplomat even arrives to help smooth the travel arrangements for him. Throughout the film, money and corpses are seen in the same terms.

Walter Matthau, Jack Lemmon and Susan Sarandon in *The Front Page* (1974).

Opposite page: Marthe Keller and William Holden in *Fedora* (1978).

Their movements are negotiated by means of blackmail, ransom demands and cunning. So this apparently sparkling romantic comedy is dark and sleazy, despite the beauty of the landscapes. The only change is that the male character becomes more human and gives in to the girl's request by agreeing to find replacements for the bodies of his father and his mistress so that they can be laid to rest on Italian soil. After this we can imagine that he will do exactly as his father did and come every summer to meet the English girl in this hotel. Like his father, he will lead a double life. In Wilder's films the good life is for the selfish.

The end of a particular idea of cinema

Hollywood changed during the 1970s. The end of censorship opened a Pandora's box and pornography poured from the screens. Audiences no longer wanted classicism. *Avanti!* was a flop.

Wilder wanted to make a hit. So he fell back on *The Front Page*, a play by Ben Hecht and

Charles McArthur that had already been adapted for the screen several times,[17] and used the duo from *The Fortune Cookie*, Jack Lemmon and Walter Matthau. *The Front Page* (1974) is a biting satire on journalism in the 1920s, while also being an apology for it. The film is formally perfect, paced for efficiency and faithful to the original play, displaying Wilder's directorial wizardry. The comic tone is joyful, but the audiences of the day were unmoved.

After producing and directing this film, Wilder swore he would never shoot another remake, but nonetheless ended his career with *Buddy Buddy* (1981), an unconvincing adaptation of a successful French film, Édouard Molinaro's *L'Emmerdeur* (1973), written by Francis Weber, in which he again brought together Lemmon and Matthau.

But this was one movie too many as, three years before, Wilder had produced and directed a wonderful film that we can legitimately regard as his cinematic testament: *Fedora* (1978).

Financed by European capital, this very free adaptation of a novel by former actor Thomas Tryon marked Wilder's return to film noir and melodrama in the spirit of *Sunset Boulevard*. The presence of William Holden reinforces the reference, as does the dramatic structure organized around flashbacks.

Pessimistic, cruel and full of disillusionment, *Fedora* is a jigsaw puzzle about death, both that of a young woman whose identity has been stolen and that of a vanished cinema that knew how to combine art with commerce. A many-layered requiem, it avoids nostalgia and sarcasm, being shot full of humanity to attain the emotional force of Vincente Minnelli's finest dramas.

The film is a bonfire of all of Wilder's perennial themes: social ambition, money, power, dressing up and role play, lies, betrayal, obsessions, vampirism, closed minds and closed spaces.

Strangely, although it is about Hollywood, *Fedora* is the most European of all his films in its treatment of its subject. Moreover, it shows America only in flashbacks linked to the film world. The rest of the story takes place in Europe, where ghosts are not just shadows on a screen.

From a soap-opera story — a disfigured actress passes her daughter off as herself in order to pursue her career — Wilder builds a magisterial film on the search for identity, madness, the death wish and the power of memories. And as he is primarily a moralist, he refuses to perpetuate legends, choosing instead to show the banal reality of film as the product of an industry whose factories churn out illusions, in the form of films and stars, along with the resulting schizophrenia. This time there's no humour. The tragedy staged here has no use for it. And this oratorio on the substitution of faces, with Rozsa's lyrical score as counterpoint, at last reveals the true face of Billy Wilder: a man who has never believed in dreams and has always suffered from the recurrent ignominy of reality.

Chronology

1906
22 June. Birth of Samuel Wilder, known as Billy, son of Max and Eugenia Wilder, at Sucha Beskidzka in Galicia, then a province of the Austro-Hungarian empire. He has an older brother, Wilhelm. His father is a railway station catering manager.

1909
The Wilders move to Vienna.

1911–24
Primary school, then high school. Wilder is an average student. His parents want him to be a doctor or a lawyer.

1916
Billy discovers that his father has an illegitimate child. He observes the funeral procession of Emperor Franz Josef.

1918
Billy's brother Wilhelm leaves for London and then New York. Billy falls in love with ten-year-old Irka Schreber.

1920
Already passionate about sport, Wilder becomes interested in jazz, theatre and literature.

1924
Leaves school and refuses to go to university.

1925
Begins working as a journalist in Vienna. Works for *Die Stunde*. Brief encounter with Sigmund Freud.

1926
Moves to Berlin, where he continues in journalism. Lives on Pariserstrasse and falls in love with a chorus girl, Olive Victoria, who does not respond to his advances.

Annie Schreyer and Brigitte Borchert in *People on Sunday* (1930).

1927
Uncredited work on various film scripts. Becomes friends with the great screenplay writer Carl Mayer.

1928
Max Wilder dies while passing through Berlin. Billy starts collecting art works and frequents the Romanisches Café. Gets himself hired as a professional dancer and gigolo at the Eden Hotel and publishes a series of humorous articles based on this experience, 'Waiter, get me a dancer!', in the *Berliner Zeitung am Mittag*.

1929
First film credit for *Hell of a Reporter*, in which he also plays a small role. Shooting of *People on Sunday*.

1930
Scriptwriting contract with UFA. Plans to make a film about the Romanisches Café.

1931–3
Writes several screenplays for commercial films and has friends among the Berlin intellectuals, particularly those linked to the Bauhaus.

1933
Leaves Nazi Germany for Paris, where he lives at the Hotel Ansonia.

Michel Duran, Raymond Galle and Pierre Mingand in *Mauvaise Graine* (1934).

1934
Directs *Mauvaise Graine* with Alexandre Esway. Goes into exile in the USA, entering the country via Mexico. Works as a screenwriter in Hollywood.

1935
Short trip to Vienna to see his mother.

1936
Marries Judith Cappicus, who is divorced with a child.

1937
Enters Paramount and starts writing with Charles Brackett.

1938
First film for Ernst Lubitsch, *Bluebeard's Eighth Wife*.

1939
His wife gives birth to twins, Victoria and Vincent. Vincent dies a few weeks later. First collaboration with Mitchell Leisen on *Midnight*. Nominated for an Oscar for Lubitsch's *Ninotchka*.

1941
Oscar nomination for Leisen's *Hold Back the Dawn* and Hawks's *Ball of Fire*, for which he was on set throughout shooting.

1942
Uncredited work on the script of Julien Duvivier's *Tales of Manhattan*. Makes his debut as a director with *The Major and the Minor*.

1943
First film with Erich von Stroheim, *Five Graves to Cairo*. Works with composer Miklos Rozsa for the first time.

Billy Wilder with Ray Milland on the set of *The Lost Weekend* (1945).

1944
Oscar nominations for the screenplay and direction of *Double Indemnity*, which Wilder wrote with Raymond Chandler and without Brackett. The film is an instant hit and wins critical acclaim.

1945
Billy's brother Wilhelm moves to Hollywood, where he produces and directs B movies under the name of William L. Wilder. Billy shoots *The Lost Weekend*. Meets Audrey Young. Travels to Germany with the army and is posted to Frankfurt. The Red Cross tells him that his entire family have been deported and exterminated at Auschwitz. Supervises the editing of *Die Todesmuhlen* (*Death Mills*), a documentary on the death camps.

1946
Divorces Judith Cappicus after a four-year separation. Oscar for direction and screenplay of *The Lost Weekend*. Ray Milland wins the Oscar for Best Actor.

1947
Uncredited work on the script of Henry Koster's *The Bishop's Wife*. Shoots *The Emperor Waltz* as a reaction against depression following his time in Europe.

1948
Oscar nomination for the screenplay of *A Foreign Affair*. Works with Marlene Dietrich for the first time in this film and allows her to do the lighting for herself.

Billy Wilder with Tom Ewell and Marilyn Monroe on the set of *The Seven Year Itch* (1955).

1949

Marries Audrey Young.

1950

Oscar for the screenplay of *Sunset Boulevard* and nomination for Best Director. Abruptly ends his collaboration with Charles Brackett. Project for a film with Laurel and Hardy.

1951

Starts producing his own films. First commercial failure with *Ace in the Hole*, despite an Oscar nomination for Best Screenplay. Paramount renames the film *The Big Carnival*.

1953

Oscar nomination for directing *Stalag 17*. William Holden wins Oscar for Best Actor. Difficulties with Paramount, who want to change the nationality of the traitor in the film. Wilder objects and gets his way.

1954

First film with Audrey Hepburn, *Sabrina*. Oscar nominations for Best Director and Best Screenplay.

1955

First film with Marilyn Monroe, *The Seven Year Itch*. Leaves Paramount.

1957

First collaboration with (uncredited) art director Alexandre Trauner on *The Spirit of St. Louis*. Begins writing with I. A. L. Diamond *on Love in the Afternoon*.

1958

Oscar nomination for Best Director for *Witness for the Prosecution*.

1959

Some Like It Hot: first film with the Mirisch Company and Associated Artists. First film with Jack Lemmon. An international hit. Oscar nominations for Best Director and Best Screenplay, but William Wyler's *Ben Hur* sweeps the board. A journalist gets their names muddled and Wilder says, 'You know, Wyler, Wilder; Manet, Monet…'

1960

First film with Shirley MacLaine, *The Apartment*. Oscars for Best Picture, Best Screenplay and Best Director. Project for a film with the Marx Brothers, *A Day at the United Nations*. Uncredited help with the screenplay for Lewis Milestone's *Ocean's Eleven*. Frank Sinatra thanks him with a Picasso drawing.

1963

Irma la Douce is a worldwide hit.

1964

Shooting on *Kiss Me, Stupid* is interrupted when Peter Sellers has a heart attack. He is replaced by Ray Walston. The film is boycotted by American decency campaigners.

1966

The Fortune Cookie flops with audiences and critics, despite Walter Matthau's Oscar for Best Supporting Actor and Wilder and Diamond's nomination for Best Screenplay. Wilder works on the script for *Casino Royale*.

1968

The Apartment is made into the musical *Promises, Promises*.

1970

The Private Life of Sherlock Holmes is butchered by Paramount. Wilder does not protest.

1973

Some Like It Hot is made into the stage musical *Sugar*.

1978

Fedora is shot using French and German finance.

1981

Wilder directs his last film, *Buddy Buddy*.

1983

Tribute to Billy Wilder at the Film Society of Lincoln Center in New York.

1985

Griffith Prize from the Directors Guild of America.

1987

Life Achievement Award from the American Film Institute.

1988

Irving-Thalberg Prize at the Oscar ceremony. Wilder's scriptwriter I. A. L. Diamond dies.

1989

Sells his painting collection for $32,600,000.

1991

Receives the Austrian Gold Medal First Class. Becomes president of the Billy Wilder Institut in Germany, to train producers and screenwriters, which he abandons two years later.

1992

Considers making *Schindler's List*.

1993

Sunset Boulevard is made into a musical. On stage to receive the Oscar for Best Foreign Film, Fernando Trueba says, 'I'd like to thank God, but I don't believe in God, so I'd like to thank Billy Wilder.'

1995

Consultant on Sidney Pollack's remake of *Sabrina*.

1996

A street is named after him in the town where he was born, now in Poland. Refuses to appear in Cameron Crowe's *Jerry Maguire*.

2002

Dies 27 March in Beverly Hills.

Billy Wilder with Tony Curtis on the set of *Some Like It Hot* (1959).

Billy Wilder on the set of *Irma la Douce* (1963).

Billy Wilder with Jack Lemmon on the set of *Irma la Douce* (1963).

Billy Wilder with Robert Stephens, Geneviève Page and Colin Blakely on the set of *The Private Life of Sherlock Holmes* (1970).

Billy Wilder on the set of *Fedora* (1978).

Filmography

Mauvaise Graine   1934

B&W. **Co-director** Alexandre Esway. **Screenplay** Max Kolpe, Hans G. Lustig, Billy Wilder. **Cinematography** Paul Cotteret, Maurice Delattre. **Production design** Robert Gys. **Music** Franz Wachsman (Franz Waxman), Allan Gray. **Producer** Georges Bernier for Compagnie Nouvelle Commerciale. **Running time** 1h 26. With Danielle Darrieux (Jeannette), Pierre Mingand (Henri Pasquier), Raymond Galle (Jean la Cravate), Paul Escoffier (Dr Pasquier).

• A young man of good family refuses to get a job and takes up with a gang of car thieves. He falls in love with a girl in the gang, comes into conflict with the leader, gets away from the police and escapes to the colonies. (British version: Herbert Mason's *The First Offence*, a.k.a. *Bad Blood*, 1936.)

The Major and the Minor   1942

B&W. **Screenplay** Edward Childs Carpenter, Charles Brackett, Billy Wilder, adapted from Edward Childs Carpenter's play *Connie Goes Home* and Fannie Kilbourne's story *Sunny Goes Home*. **Cinematography** Leo Tover. **Editing** Doane Harrison. **Production design** Roland Anderson, Hans Dreier. **Music** Robert Emmett Dolan. **Production** Arthur Hornblow, Jr, for Paramount. **Running time** 1h 40. With Ginger Rogers (Susan Applegate), Ray Milland (Major Philip Kirby), Rita Johnson (Pamela Hill), Robert Benchley (Mr Osborne), Diana Lynn (Lucy Hill), Edward Fielding (Colonel Hill), Lela E. Rogers (Susan's mother).

• A young woman pretends to be a teenager to buy a cheap train ticket. A major lets her stay in his sleeping car, then takes her to a military school. He is attracted to her without realizing her true age. After a series of misunderstandings, he discovers the truth. (Remake: Norman Taurog's *You're Never Too Young*, 1955, with Jerry Lewis and Dean Martin.)

Five Graves to Cairo   1943

B&W. **Screenplay** Charles Brackett, Billy Wilder, adapted from Lajos Biro's play *Hôtel Impérial*. **Cinematography** John Seitz. **Production design** Ernst Fegté, Hans Dreier, Bertram C. Granger. **Editing** Doane Harrison. **Music** Miklos Rozsa. **Production** Charles Brackett, for Paramount. **Running time** 1h 36. With Franchot Tone (Corporal John J. Bramble), Anne Baxter (Mouche), Akim Tamiroff (Farid), Fortunio Bonanova (General Sebastiano), Peter Van Eyck (Lieutenant Schwegler), Erich von Stroheim (Field Marshal Rommel).

• British corporal Bramble takes refuge in a hotel occupied by the Germans and pretends to be a Nazi spy in order to find out what Rommel is planning. He is discovered, but saved by the self-sacrifice of the waitress, Mouche.

Double Indemnity   1944

B&W. **Screenplay** Raymond Chandler, Billy Wilder, adapted from James M. Cain's short story 'Double Indemnity' in *Three of a Kind*. **Cinematography** John Seitz. **Production design** Hal Pereira, Hans Dreier, Bertram Granger. **Editing** Doane Harrison. **Music** Miklos Rozsa. **Production** Buddy G. DeSylva and Joseph Sistrom for Paramount. **Running time** 1h 47. With Fred MacMurray (Walter Neff), Barbara Stanwyck (Phyllis Dietrichson), Edward G. Robinson (Barton Keyes), Porter Hall (M. Jackson), Jean Heather (Lola Dietrichson), Tom Powers (M. Dietrichson), Byron Barr (Nino).

• An insurance salesman devises a plan to murder his mistress's husband and receive a big payout. Everything goes according to plan, but his accomplice betrays him and he confesses to the crime.

The Lost Weekend   1945

B&W. **Screenplay** Charles Brackett, Billy Wilder, adapted from Charles R. Jackson's novel. **Cinematography** John Seitz. **Production design** Earl Hedrick, Bertram Granger, Hans Dreier. **Editing** Doane Harrison. **Music** Miklos Rozsa. **Production** Charles Brackett for Paramount. **Running time** 1h 39. With Ray Milland (Don Birman), Jane Wyman (Helen), Philip Terry (Wick), Howard Da Silva (the barman), Doris Dowling (Gloria).

• An alcoholic writer spends a weekend alone and experiences delirium tremens for the first time.

The Emperor Waltz   1948

Screenplay Charles Brackett, Billy Wilder. **Cinematography** George Barnes. **Production design** Sam Comer, Franz Bachelin, Paul Huldschinsky, Hans Dreier. **Editing** Doane Harrison. **Music** Victor Young. **Songs** Johnny Burke and Jimmy Van Heusen. **Production** Charles Brackett for Paramount. **Running time** 1h 46. With Bing Crosby (Virgil Smith), Joan Fontaine (Johanna Augusta Franziska), Richard Haydn (the Emperor), Sig Ruman (Dr Zwieback).

• Around 1900, an American tries to sell a gramophone to the Austrian emperor. He falls in love with an aristocratic girl and breaks all conventions to marry her.

A Foreign Affair   1948

B&W. **Screenplay** Charles Brackett, Richard L. Breen, Billy Wilder, from an idea by David Shaw. **Cinematography** Charles B. Lang Jr. **Production design** Sam Comer, Ross Dowd, Walter Tyler, Hans Dreier. **Editing** Doane Harrison. **Music** Frederik Hollander. **Production** Charles Brackett for Paramount. **Running time** 1h 56. With Jean Arthur (Phoebe Frost), Marlene Dietrich (Erika von Schlütow), John Lund (Captain John Pringle), Millard Mitchell (Colonel Plummer), Peter von Zerneck (Birgel), Frederik Hollander (the pianist).

• An American officer stationed in Berlin is in love with a former Nazi. He decides to protect her by seducing an American congresswoman who is investigating her, but ends up falling in love with the American.

Sunset Boulevard   1950

B&W. **Screenplay** Charles Brackett, D. M. Marsham Jr, Billy Wilder, adapted from *A Can of Beans* by Charles Brackett and Billy Wilder. **Cinematography** John Seitz. **Production design** Sam Comer, John Meehan, Ray Moyer, Hans Dreier. **Editing** Doane Harrison, Arthur Schmidt. **Music** Franz Waxman. **Production** Charles Brackett for Paramount. **Running time** 1h 50. With William Holden (Joe Gillis), Gloria Swanson (Norma Desmond), Erich von Stroheim (Max von Mayerling), Nancy Olson (Betty Schaefer), Fred Clarke (Sheldrake), Cecil B. DeMille, Hedda Hopper, Buster Keaton, H. B. Warner.

• An unscrupulous young screenwriter becomes the gigolo of a star of the silent screen, who goes mad and kills him when he tries to leave her.

Ace in the Hole / The Big Carnival   1951

B&W. **Screenplay** Walter Newman, Lesser Samuels, Billy Wilder. **Cinematography** Charles B. Lang, Jr. **Production design** Sam Comer, Hal Pereira, Ray Moyer, Earl Hedrick. **Editing** Arthur Schmidt. **Music** Hugo Friedhofer. **Production** Billy Wilder for Paramount. **Running time** 1h 51. With Kirk Douglas (Charles Tatum), Jan Sterling (Lorraine Minosa), Robert Arthur (Herbie Cook), Richard Benedict (Leo Minosa).

• A journalist cynically and hypocritically exploits a minor news story (a man buried under a mountain), but is shot by the man's greedy wife and dies without profiting from his machinations.

Stalag 17   1953

B&W. **Screenplay** Edwin Blum, Billy Wilder, adapted from a play by Donald Bevan and Edmund Trzcinski. **Cinematography** Ernest Laszlo. **Production design** Sam Comer, Hal Pereira, Ray Moyer, Franz Bachelin. **Editing** George Tomasini, Doane Harrison. **Music** Franz Waxman. **Production** Billy Wilder for Paramount. **Running time** 2h. With William Holden (Sefton), Don Taylor (Dunbar), Otto Preminger (Von Scherbach), Robert Strauss (Kasava), Harvey Lembeck (Shapiro), Richard Erdman (Hoffy), Peter Graves (Price), Sig Ruman (Schulz).

• Sefton, an individualistic prisoner of war, exploits his fellow prisoners, who suspect him of being a German spy. But he unmasks the traitor and helps a rich lieutenant to escape, hoping to get money from him.

Sabrina   1954

B&W. **Screenplay** Ernest Lehman, Billy Wilder, adapted from Samuel Taylor's play *Sabrina Fair*. **Cinematography** Charles B. Lang Jr. **Production design** Sam Comer, Hal Pereira, Ray Moyer, Walter Tyler. **Editing** Arthur Schmidt, Doane Harrison. **Music** Frederik Hollander. **Production** Billy Wilder for Paramount. **Running time** 1h 53. With Humphrey Bogart (Linus Larrabee), Audrey Hepburn (Sabrina Fairchild), William Holden (David Larrabee), Walter Hampden (Oliver Larrabee), John Williams (Thomas Fairchild), Martha Hyer (Elizabeth Tyson), Marcel Dalio (the baron).

• Sabrina dreams of marrying David, the younger son of her father's employers. To prevent such a mismatch, David's older brother pretends to be in love with the girl, but then falls in love with her for real.

The Seven Year Itch   1955

Screenplay George Axelrod, Billy Wilder, adapted from Axelrod's play.

Cinematography Milton Krasner. **Production design** George W. Davis, Lyle Wheeler, Stuart A. Reiss, Walter M. Scott. **Editing** Hugh S. Fowler. **Music** Alfred Newman. **Production** Charles K. Feldman, Doane Harrison, Billy Wilder for Twentieth Century-Fox. **Running time** 1h 45. With Marilyn Monroe (the neighbour), Tom Ewell (Richard Sherman), Evelyn Keyes (Helen Sherman), Oskar Homolka (Brubaker), Marguerite Chapman (Miss Morris).

• A married man is spending the summer alone in New York and meets a pretty blonde who is temporarily living in the apartment below. He is tempted to seduce her and behaves in a crazy way but nothing happens between them.

The Spirit of St. Louis 1957

Screenplay Wendell Mayes, Charles Lederer, Billy Wilder, adapted from Charles Lindbergh's book. **Cinematography** Robert Burks, J. Peverell Marley, Tom Tutwiler. **Production design** Art Loel, William L. Kuehl, Alexandre Trauner (uncredited). **Editing** Arthur Schmidt. **Music** Franz Waxman. **Production** Leland Hayward for Warner Bros. **Running time** 2h 15. With James Stewart (Charles Lindbergh), Murray Hamilton (Bud Gurney), Patricia Smith (young woman who gives her mirror), Bartlett Robinson (Mahoney).

• Charles Lindbergh flies across the Atlantic and remembers various episodes from his life, all linked to his desire to be the first to fly non-stop to Europe from America.

Love in the Afternoon 1957

B&W. **Screenplay** I. A. L. Diamond, Billy Wilder, after Claude Anet's *Ariane, jeune fille russe*. **Cinematography** William C. Mellor. **Production design** Alexandre Trauner. **Editing** Léonide Azar. **Music** Franz Waxman. **Production** Billy Wilder for United Artists. **Running time** 2h 10. With Gary Cooper (Frank Flannagan), Audrey Hepburn (Ariane), Maurice Chevalier (Claude Chavasse).

• Ariane pretends to live the life of

a libertine to attract an American millionaire famous for his amorous escapades.

Witness for the Prosecution   1957

B&W. **Screenplay** Harry Kurnitz, Larry Marcus, Billy Wilder, adapted from Agatha Christie's play. **Cinematography** Russell Harlan. **Production design** Alexandre Trauner. **Costumes** Edith Head. **Editing** Daniel Mandell. **Music** Matty Malneck. **Song** 'I May Never Go Home Anymore' by Jack Brooks, Ralph Arthur Robert. **Production** Edward Small and Arthur Hornblow, Jr, for Theme Pictures. **Running time** 1h 56. With Tyrone Power (Leonard), Marlene Dietrich (Christine), Charles Laughton (Sir Wilfrid Robarts), Elsa Lanchester (the nurse).

• A lawyer who obtains the acquittal of a man accused of murder discovers he has been manipulated.

Some Like It Hot   1959

B&W. **Screenplay** I. A. L. Diamond, Billy Wilder, from a story by Robert Thoeren and Michael Logan. **Cinematography** Charles Lang Jr. **Production design** Ted Haworth, Edward G. Boyle. **Editing** Arthur P. Schmidt. **Music** Adolph Deutsch. **Songs** A. H. Gibbs, Gus Kahn, Bert Kalmar, Herbert Stothart, Leo Wood. **Production** Billy Wilder for Mirisch Company. **Running time** 2h. With Marilyn Monroe (Sugar), Tony Curtis (Joe), Jack Lemmon (Jerry), George Raft (Colombo), Pat O'Brien (Mulligan), Joe E. Brown (Osgood Fielding III).

• Having witnessed a gangland massacre, two musicians are pursued by gangsters and escape by disguising themselves as women in a big band travelling to Florida. One of them falls in love with the singer, Sugar, while the other is wooed by a millionaire. Discovered by the gangsters, they escape with the millionaire and the singer.

The Apartment   1960

B&W. **Screenplay** I. A. L. Diamond, Billy Wilder. **Cinematography** Joseph LaShelle. **Editing** Daniel Mandell. **Production design** Alexandre Trauner. **Music** Adolph Deutsch. **Production** Billy Wilder for Mirisch Company. **Running time** 2h 05. With Jack Lemmon (Calvin Clifford Baxter), Shirley MacLaine (Fran Kubelik), Fred MacMurray (Jeff Sheldrake), Ray Walston (Dobisch).

• A man lends his apartment to his office superiors to meet their mistresses until the day when the company boss asks him for this service. The employee is rewarded by spectacular promotion, but discovers that the boss is having an affair with the woman he is secretly in love with. The woman tries to kill herself in his apartment. He saves her, refuses to go on lending out the premises, loses his job and finds love with the woman.

One, Two, Three   1961

B&W. **Screenplay** I. A. L. Diamond, Billy Wilder, adapted from a play by Ferenc Molnár. **Cinematography** Daniel L. Fapp. **Production design** Alexandre Trauner. **Editing** Daniel Mandell. **Music** André Prévin. **Production** Billy Wilder for Mirisch Company, Pyramid. **Running time** 1h 55. With James Cagney (MacNamara), Horst Buchholz (Otto Ludwig-Piffl), Pamela Tiffin (Scarlett), Arlene Francis (Madame MacNamara), Liselotte Pulver (Ingeborg).

• The head of Coca-Cola in Berlin, who is trying to break into the Soviet market, is caught up in a difficult situation when his boss's daughter marries a communist. To keep his job he works flat out to turn the Bolshevik into a capitalist aristocrat.

Irma la Douce   1963

Screenplay I. A. L. Diamond, Billy Wilder, adapted from Alexandre Breffort's play. **Cinematography** Joseph LaShelle. **Production**

design Alexandre Trauner. **Editing** Daniel Mandell. **Music** Marguerite Monnot, André Prévin. **Production** Billy Wilder for Mirisch Company, Phalanx. **Running time** 2h 27. With Jack Lemmon (Nestor Patou), Shirley MacLaine (Irma), Lou Jacobi (Moustache), Bruce Yarnell (Hippolyte).

• A Paris policeman becomes an unwilling pimp for a woman whom he wants to stop selling herself to men. He pretends to be a rich, impotent lord and becomes her only client. This strategy obliges him to take clandestine work at the market of Les Halles. He is exhausted and fakes his double's drowning, but is then accused of his murder.

Kiss Me, Stupid   1964
B&W. **Screenplay** I. A. L. Diamond, Billy Wilder, adapted from Anna Bonacci's play *L'Ora della fantasia*. **Cinematography** Joseph LaShelle. **Production design** Alexandre Trauner. **Editing** Daniel Mandell. **Music** George Gershwin, André Prévin. **Production** Billy Wilder for Mirisch Company, Phalanx. **Running time** 2h 40. With Dean Martin (Dino), Kim Novak (Polly), Ray Walston (Orville J. Spooner), Felicia Farr (Zelda), Cliff Osmond (Barney Millsap).

• A pair of songwriters detain a Las Vegas star in their small town so they can sell him songs, and pay a prostitute to take the place of one of their wives and 'be nice' to him. But nothing goes according to plan and the star sleeps with the man's real wife, thinking she's a prostitute. All the same, he adds one of their songs to his repertoire.

The Fortune Cookie   1966
B&W. **Screenplay** I. A. L. Diamond, Billy Wilder. **Cinematography** Joseph LaShelle. **Production design** Edward G. Boyle. **Editing** Daniel Mandell. **Music** André Previn. **Production** Billy Wilder for Mirish Company, Phalanx. **Running time** 2h 05. With Jack Lemmon (Hinkle), Walter Matthau (Gingrich), Ron Rich (Boom Boom), Judi West (Sandy), Cliff Osmond (Purkey).

• After an accident at a sports ground, a cameraman is persuaded by his brother-in-law (a crooked lawyer) to pretend to be paralysed in order to receive a big insurance payout. The football player responsible for the accident is not in on the plot and looks after the man he thinks is his victim. Sickened and aware that he has been tricked, the cameraman abandons the act.

The Private Life of Sherlock Holmes   1970
Screenplay I. A. L. Diamond, Billy Wilder, based on Conan Doyle's characters. **Cinematography** Christopher Challis. **Production design** Alexandre Trauner. **Editing** Ernest Walter. **Music** Miklos Rozsa. **Production** Billy Wilder for Mirisch Company, Phalanx. **Running time** 2h 05. With Robert Stephens (Holmes), Colin Blakely (Watson), Geneviève Page (Gabrielle), Christopher Lee (Mycroft), Clive Revill (Rogozhin).

• Having declined a proposition to get a great Russian ballet dancer pregnant, Holmes investigates the disappearance of Suzanne Valadon's husband. He, Suzanne and Watson go to Scotland, where Mycroft Holmes tells his brother that his client is a German spy who is manipulating him.

Avanti!   1972
Screenplay I. A. L. Diamond, Billy Wilder, adapted from Samuel Taylor's play. **Cinematography** Luigi Kuveiller. **Production design** Fernandino Scarfiotti. **Editing** Ralph E. Winters. **Music** Carlo Rustichelli. **Production** Billy Wilder for Mirisch Company, Phalanx, Jalem. **Running time** 2h 24. With Jack Lemmon (Wendell Armbruster), Juliet Mills (Pamela Piggott), Clive Revill (Carlo Carlucci), Edwards Andrews Jr (Blodgett).

• Following his father's death in Italy, an American businessman travels to the country and discovers that his father had for several years been conducting an affair there with an English woman, whose daughter

has also turned up. In the end he falls in love with her and continues his father's tradition by becoming her lover.

The Front Page   1974
Screenplay Ben Hecht, Charles McArthur, I. A. L. Diamond, Billy Wilder. **Cinematography** Jordan S. Cronenweth. **Production design** Henry Bumstead. **Costumes** Burton Miller. **Editing** Ralph E. Winters. **Production** Paul Monash, Billy Wilder for Universal. **Running time** 1h 45. With Jack Lemmon (Hildy), Walter Matthau (Burns), Susan Sarandon (Peggy), Vincent Gardenia (The sheriff), David Wayne (Bensinger), Allen Garfield (Kruger), Austin Pendleton (Earl Williams), Charles Durning (Murphy), Harold Gould (The mayor), Cliff Osmond (The policeman).

• A journalist gives up his work to marry the girl he loves, but his editor-in-chief strives to prevent the marriage by any means possible.

Fedora   1978
Screenplay I. A. L. Diamond, Billy Wilder, adapted from Thomas Tryon's novel *Crowned Heads*. **Cinematography** Gerry Fisher. **Production design** Alexandre Trauner. **Editing** Stefan Arnsten, Fredric Steinkamp. **Music** Miklos Rozsa. **Production** Billy Wilder for Bavaria Atelier GmbH (Germany) and SFP France. **Running time** 1h 54. With William Holden (Dutch), Marthe Keller (Antonia), Hildegard Knef (Countess Sobriansky), José Ferrer (Vando), Henry Fonda, Michael York.

• An independent American producer wants to meet the star Fedora to bring her back to the screen and discovers the secret of her youthfulness. She is actually the daughter of the real Fedora, who was disfigured by cell rejuvenation treatment.

Buddy Buddy   1981
Screenplay Francis Weber, I. A. L. Diamond, Billy Wilder. **Cinematography** Harry Sradling, Jr. **Production design** Daniel A. Lomino. **Editing** Argyle Nelson. **Music** Lalo Schifrin. **Production** Jay Weston for MGM. **Running time** 1h 36. With Jack Lemmon (Clooney), Walter Matthau (Trabucco), Paula Prentiss (Celia), Klaus Kinski (Zuckerbrot), Dana Elcar (Hubris), Miles Chapin (the bellhop).

• A hitman is harassed by a desperate man who stops him carrying out his contract.

Selected Bibliography

Richard Armstrong,
Billy Wilder, American Film Realist,
McFarland, Jefferson, NC, 2000.

Charlotte Chandler,
*Nobody's Perfect: Billy Wilder,
a Personal Biography*,
Simon & Schuster, New York,
2002.

Cameron Crowe,
Conversations with Wilder,
Alfred A. Knopf, New York, 2004.

Gene D. Phillips,
*Some Like It Wilder: The Life
and Controversial Films of Billy
Wilder*, Screen Classics series,
University Press of Kentucky,
Lexington, 2009.

Ed Sikov,
*On Sunset Boulevard: The Life
and Times of Billy Wilder*,
Hyperion, New York, 1998.

Notes

1. Burt Prelutsky, 'An Interview with Billy Wilder', *Michigan Quarterly Review* (Winter 1996).

2. Expressionism, an artistic movement promoted by the German magazine *Der Sturm* just before World War I, used subjective distortions of reality to provoke an emotive sense of strangeness in the viewer. It influenced painting, literature, architecture, theatre and also German silent cinema.

3. Hervé Dumont, *Robert Siodmak, le maître du film noir*, Éditions L'Âge d'Homme, Lausanne, 1981.

4. Universum Film Aktiengesellschaft, a film production and distribution company.

5. Words taken from the film, *Billy Wilder, Portrait of a 60 % Perfect Man*, by Annie Tresgot, 1980.

6. Cecil B. DeMille (1881–1959) was an American director who started his career in the days of silent cinema. Billy Wilder gave him a part in *Sunset Boulevard*. Ernst Lubitsch (1892–1947) was an American director of German origin who started out as an actor for theatre director Max Reinhardt before making big-budget films in Germany. After moving to Hollywood in 1923, he rose to prominence as a major director specializing in comedy. Josef von Sternberg (1894–1969) was an American director of Austrian origin. He started out in Hollywood in 1925 and made *The Blue Angel* (1930) in Germany, introducing Marlene Dietrich, whom he then brought to America.

7. Interview with Jean Domarchi and Jean Douchet, *Cahiers du cinéma*, 134 (August 1962).

8. James Mallahan Cain (1892–1977) was an American journalist, screenwriter and novelist. He wrote *The Postman Always Rings Twice* and *Mildred Pierce*.

9. Raymond Thornton Chandler (1888–1959) wrote crime novels and screenplays. He was the creator of private detective Philip Marlowe.

10. *The Blue Angel* (1930), a German film by Josef von Sternberg (1894–1969), was the film in which Marlene Dietrich first came to prominence.

11. Jacques Doniol-Valcroze, 'Les métamorphoses cruelles', *Cahiers du cinéma*, 45 (March 1955).

12. Cameron Crowe, *Conversations with Wilder*, Alfred A. Knopf, New York, 2001, p.89.

13. Charles Laughton (1899–1962), British actor and director of one film: *The Night of the Hunter* (1955).

14. Cameron Crowe, *Conversations with Wilder*, p. 152.

15. Ferenc Molnár (1878–1952), Hungarian playwright and author of *Liliom*, adapted for the screen by Fritz Lang in 1934.

16. Interview with Michel Ciment, *Positif*, 155 (January 1974).

17. *The Front Page* had previously been adapted by Lewis Milestone (*The Front Page*, 1931) and Howard Hawks (*His Girl Friday*, 1940).

Sources

Collection BIFI: p.97 (2nd col. bottom, 3rd col.)
Collection Cahiers du cinéma: cover, inside front cover–p.1, pp.2–3, 4–5, 9, 14, 18–9, 20, 21, 22–3, 25, 26–7, 28, 30, 32–3, 36, 40, 41, 42–3, 44–5, 46, 47, 50–1, 52, 57, 68, 70–1, 72, 73, 76, 78, 82–3, 84, 86–7,

97 (2nd col. top).
Collection Cahiers du cinéma/D. Rabourdin: pp.53, 54, 54–5, 56, 58–9, 60–1, 62–3, 64, 67, 69, 74–5, 79, 85, 92, 97 (1st col.), 103, 104–inside back cover.
Collection CAT'S: pp.15, 16–7, 48–9, 77,

80–1, 88, 94–5.
Collection Cinémathèque française: pp.11, 13, 34–5, 38–9, 65, 90, 91, 93, 94–5.
Filmandriv Gerhard Lamprecht Berlin: p.10.
Collection RMN: p.8.
Screen grabs: pp.31, 37, 66.

Credits

Opposite page: Tony Curtis on the set of *Some Like It Hot* (1959).
Cover: Marilyn Monroe in *Some Like It Hot* (1959).
Inside front cover: Billy Wilder on the set of *Irma la Douce* (1963).
Inside back cover: Gary Cooper and Audrey Hepburn in *Love in the Afternoon* (1957).

Cahiers du cinéma Sarl
65, rue Montmartre
75002 Paris

www.cahiersducinema.com

Revised edition © 2011 Cahiers du cinéma Sarl
First published in French as *Billy Wilder* © 2007 Cahiers du cinéma Sarl

ISBN 978 2 8664 2609 5

Series conceived by Claudine Paquot
Concept designed by Werner Jeker/Les Ateliers du Nord
Designed by Pascaline Richir
Translated by Trista Selous
Printed in China

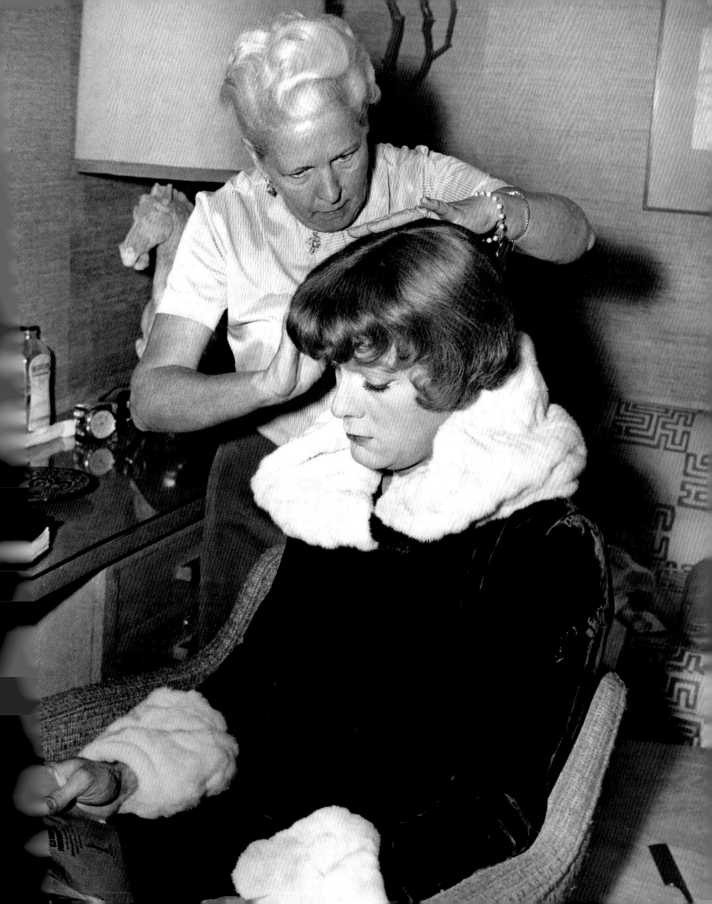